Awakening Woman

Marie-Louise von Franz, Honorary Patron

**Studies in Jungian Psychology
by Jungian Analysts**

Daryl Sharp, General Editor

CONTENTS

See final pages for descriptions of other Inner City Books

Introduction

> In each of us there is another whom we do not know. {She] speaks
> to us in dreams and tells us how differently [she] sees us from the
> way we see ourselves. When, therefore, we find ourselves in a diffi-
> cult situation to which there is no solution, [she] can sometimes
> kindle a light that radically alters our attitude—the very attitude that
> led us into the difficult situation.[1]

This book tells the story of a woman's growing consciousness and the
far-reaching aspects of womanhood she came to know. It describes
the way her dreams led her to this new consciousness and inner
strength. One might say it is a mystery, for it details the unraveling of
dark, intimate clues that methodically arose from the unconscious in
the form of archetypal images. The symbolism found in dream material was the guiding factor in clarifying those facets of life which had
been denied a role in her conscious life.

This is also a story of feminine sexuality. It tells of the repression
this woman experienced in her culture, family and religion that all
suggested what an admirable woman "should" be. Through her dreams,
a new image emerged—the dark-haired woman. This image enabled
her to redeem her connection with the fullness of feminine nature
that had lain dormant in her most of her life.

Actually, it was the dreams of both this woman and myself—the
analysand and the analyst—that brought her story to book form.
Leila, as we shall call her—the name itself means "dark-haired
woman"—had this dream several years after she began analysis:

> I was seated in a large open room across from an analyst. Apart from us,
> sitting in a semicircle, were three female cousins (who in real life were

---

[1] "The Meaning of Psychology in Modern Man," *Civilization in Transition,* CW 10,
par. 325. [CW refers throughout to *The Collected Works of C.G. Jung]*

stereotypes of myself). The analyst requests that I tell them my dream, for it was something these women needed to know. When I refused he said in a definite tone, "If you do not tell the dream, the priest cannot come."

I decide to share: I say: I dream that I am in a laboratory of some kind. I see a woman who is in a large flask suspended in bubbling water. She is like a caricature of Marilyn Monroe with platinum blonde wig, bright red rouged cheeks and lips. A man drains her of blood and fills her with air. She was being kept alive but bloated from being underwater. A powerful voice says, "It began when she was one. What it didn't take into account is that sometimes the psyche rises up and defends itself."

The dream within the dream spoke of a woman grotesquely suspended, as if she were some mad-scientist's concoction, a "test-tube" case, as it were. And yes, this is the image many women of all generations are influenced by from "year one." The dreamer is instructed to enlighten the other women about this misshapen image. Leila described the three women as living only to be pretty, sociable and charming—the same value system passed down to herself. On a subjective level, the dream alarmed Leila with the hideous image she was unconsciously fostering. However, there was some comfort in knowing that the self-regulating psychic process was healthy and active (defending itself).

On an objective level, what did it mean that she had to tell others of the artificially painted and bloated imitation of life? So that women tightly bound in collective thinking would also come to recognize it within themselves? Did it mean, as the dream analyst said, that "the priest couldn't come"—meaning that a spiritual understanding (consciousness) for herself and other women could not come about until this occurred? How concrete does "telling" have to be? It was as if a challenge had been issued, but Leila was unable to respond to it at that time.

A month or so later, I had a dream in which I was holding a book I had written, entitled *A Woman's Awakening.* The following morning, not having recalled the dream, images of Leila kept occurring to me, so much that I wondered if some grievous harm had come to her. This was unusual for me. Then in an instant, the dream flashed into consciousness and I knew that *A Woman's Awakening* was related to Leila and her analysis. I wondered how concrete "the book" was, or if it pointed more to the symbolism of the analytic process.

Certainly, Leila was a woman who was awakening from a comatose psychic state. But my conscious mind already knew this. Why would the unconscious remind me of it? Had I once seen such a title in a bookstore but somehow registered it only subliminally? Should I take the image metaphorically as "my work," or as an actual book? These questions were left unanswered, but not unheeded.

Two months later, on New Year's Eve, Leila had this dream:

> My husband and I are visiting a couple I knew in the first years of our marriage. A strange woman squeezed into my chair with me, her back to me. She turned to face me, with eyes unlike anything I've ever seen. One looked upward and the other downward. She told me that I should write *my* mystery story. Another woman, one who is usually bed-ridden, walks toward me. She is dressed in a long maidenly night gown. She hands me a large fish, still alive with its mouth wide open. It won't close its mouth. I walk down a steep staircase carrying the fish in my arms.

Leila realized that the couple was just like herself and her husband: the man was a successful breadwinner and the wife was sweet and charming. The wife had no identity other than as her husband's spouse. Yet unusual events happen in this ordinary setting. The woman, who is a stranger, is described as an average person except for the positioning of the eyes. It was as if her sight was not focused on what was directly in front of her, but on that which came from above and below. Our mental image of the psyche generally places consciousness above and the unconscious below. It was as if this dream woman had her sight focused on both places at the same time— conscious outer life and unconscious inner life.

When I asked what she imagined her mystery to be, Leila responded after much consideration, "I am the mystery, a mystery to myself. The story is the mystery of my inner life."

In the dream, the woman in a maiden's gown represented an aspect of Leila which had never matured psychologically. This was the illness rendering her a bed-ridden invalid who could not attend to herself. The maiden woman relinquishes the large fish, still alive, yet gasping for breath. The fish is a common symbol of the early Church, and Christ was called *Ichthys*, meaning fish. This symbol of the roots of Christianity cannot survive an immature approach to Christianity. The fish must be returned to the seas of the unconscious in order for life to continue. The fish also suggests life in abundance, and indeed, fertility is a characteristic of the deep unconscious. Leila, with the element of new reality entrusted to her, leaves behind her identification with the images of the good wife and the invalid maiden. She descends the perilous steps alone.

Dreams that occur on special days such as holidays and birthdays often relate to specific aspects of the dreamer's psyche which are connected to that day. As this dream occurred on New Year's Eve, possibly it spoke of something new beginning in the following year. At the same time it presented the question of how literally to take the advice to "write" her story.

Leila was conscientious in keeping her personal journal. She recorded not simply daily events but insights, memories and moods. These were always connected to the dreams of the previous night. She was writing—what more did the dream woman with unusual eyes want of her? Did writing mean publishing a book which told of her journey into the unconscious and her dream work? Was this the way to reacquire her life force? That was a frightening thought, leaving Leila feeling very exposed and vulnerable. Yet the question of telling her story had to be addressed.

Something I rarely do is to tell my dream of an analysand to that person. Yet I felt a strong urge to share with Leila my dream of *A Woman's Awakening*. Aware that this might complicate our analytic work, I chose to do so anyway. My prevailing feelings were related to the wonder of two psyches working in parallel, almost as in a dance.

We spoke of the possible dangers in hushed tones, as if in sacred space. We discussed the change in our relationship if together we started a project of writing the mystery of a woman's analysis as seen through her dreams. It felt daunting yet fitting, though we both knew that the details were still unclear.

Often when there is doubt about proceeding in a given situation, it is important to take a conscious stand and let the unconscious respond. This is what we did, and the unconscious sent a dream to Leila that seemed to support our decision to go ahead:

> I walk toward a church and see that the doors of the sanctuary are open. I see the slender straight backs of several white-haired and properly hatted women as they enter the church. They all look alike. I take a side path that leads behind the church. There is another small sanctuary there. A handsome white-haired priest, vested for worship, comes out and shakes my hand warmly. He says, "I am fascinated with what you're doing." Inside the small sanctuary I am dumbfounded to observe that my writing table is set up at the altar. The black loose-leaf notebook I use for journaling and the book *Alone of All Her Sex* is open on the table. Others mill about as if waiting for something to happen. I sit and look at my worn-out sneaker; nervously I pull on the tongue of the sneaker. I feel awkward about what I'm doing. Others enter as if for a worship service. I decide that the only thing I can do is to continue with my writing.

Now the priest could come and offer words of encouragement. The writing now serves a higher meaning. The personal journal is placed beside a most instructive book by Marina Warner about the myths and cult of the Virgin Mary, a subject which later became prominent in Leila's dream life. Although there is a feeling of awkwardness and hesitation, there is strong support from the psyche to continue writing the story of her mystery.

These are the events, psychological and personal, that led to the writing of this book. Each chapter is headed by one of Leila's dreams. Although she had literally hundreds in the course of our work together, we have chosen those we think best tell of her developing relationship with the unconscious, the symbolic meaning of the dark-haired woman and how Leila consciously integrated this image.

I have written from the analyst's perspective, giving the dream interpretations along with Leila's associations to the images. My commentary is in plain type. Leila has contributed the personal side of the story, based on her daily journal. She has detailed her reactions, memories and insights as they transpired around the time of each dream. Her voice is written in *italics.*

Leila's dreams are interpreted here in terms of the Jungian model of the psyche. Her dream images arise from her personal psychology, but they also have an archetypal dimension in that they correspond to universal images common to all humankind. Amplification with archetypal material from myths, fairy tales and religious symbolism is presented in order to understand the images as fully as possible. This book focuses on dreams as gifts from the unconscious that support body and soul, bringing new life. It does not explore the depth and intensity of the dialectical process or the therapeutic alliance.

Though this is the account of one person's journey into the uncharted world of the unconscious, it parallels the journeys of many others. Of course, Leila's personal history and circumstances are unique to her, but there are many aspects of her story that are universal. We will encounter many "characters" that peopled Leila's dreams—animals, space men, dwarfs, the Virgin Mary and the recurring image of the dark-haired woman. They represent different aspects of herself. A reader may not have had identical dream images, but her or his dream "characters" also represent other sides of themselves seeking acknowledgment.

Leila's cultural background may be slightly or vastly different from that of any given reader, but there will still be connections between their experiences. The basic question to ask oneself is: "What are the imposed boundaries, imagined limitations or unrealistic fears that prevent me from experiencing life to the full?"

The answer, or answers, to this question is the essence of what Jung called the path of individuation.

1
The Dawn of Awakening

When opening the door for a new analysand I always wonder who it is that Fate has sent, what our connection will be, what we will learn from each other. And so it was with Leila.

All stereotypical depictions of what comprises a "Southern Lady" seemed to be embodied in this middle-aged woman. I too was raised in the Southern ways of life and was very familiar with her genteel demeanor. Leila had a quiet, well-modulated voice, and a certain frailty. Her shoulders were slightly bent, as one sees in depression, and she wore a subdued print with a lace collar. Her naturally blonde hair was close to her face, and she used a minimum of cosmetics. Hers was a delicate beauty, yet her gaze was expressionless except for deep sorrow around the eyes. The clear, lineless face did not reveal the experiences of her fifty years. Her hands were demurely folded; her feet in low-heel pumps were crossed at the ankles. Everything about her seemed subtly controlled, as if she were afraid of calling attention to herself. At times she had a faraway look. There was a certain charm, a gentleness about her, but her sadness pervaded everything.

Leila reminded me of the women of my mother's generation, gathered together for iced tea on a summer afternoon. It was as if time had stopped for her thirty or forty years ago. Like Sleeping Beauty she had been asleep or unconscious. She was unaware of herself as an individual and walked through life as if enacting a role. She moved mechanically through the motions of daily affairs and interactions with others, without a deep-seated connection. I sensed a strong, protective wall around her. Like the fairy tale princess asleep in the tower she was psychologically immature, still a maiden.

Leila came into analysis because of a long history of depression. I was told that seven years earlier she had experienced a psychological breakdown. Antidepressants were prescribed, and under the care of a psychiatrist she maintained a semblance of balance in daily life. Leila related to me that as desperate as she was, ironically it was the pain of her depression which gave her a feeling of acceptance. Fervently participating in church circles, she witnessed about her faith in healing. Her image of herself was one of piety, to the point of considering herself monastic. Her depression was constantly reinforced by others, who commented on how bravely she carried her heavy burden.

At the time I first saw Leila, she and her husband were also seeing a marriage counselor. They had serious problems: lack of sensitivity, loss of expressed affection, miscommunications and so on, but continued their roles of husband and wife as if by rote. Leila related that her husband was supportive but did not understand why she was depressed. She grew ever more fearful that he could not last as the stable factor in her life. It was at the psychiatrist's suggestion that she sought analysis, as she seemed to be looking for something more than just how to maintain old patterns. Her dreams were flooding her with images that could only be understood symbolically, which required an approach different from the medical model. The depression persisted (albeit eased by the medication) and there was a growing concern about the possibility of anorexia.

As with any analysand who is chronically depressed (that is, experiencing more than the usual down times of everyday life), I asked myself, what does the depression want us to know? What is consciousness afraid of?

I put these questions to Leila as I explained that depression has meaning and, as a symptom, alerts one to some psychological wound. The amount of psychic energy required to literally keep unacceptable images or ideas "depressed" and distant from consciousness can be enormous, to the point that it robs physical energy usually available for other activities.

To illustrate, I asked her to imagine the amount of physical strength required to keep a door tightly shut against invaders. Our psychological life is similar. Any fantasy or thought deemed incompatible with our conscious image of ourselves, or incongruous with our conscious beliefs or attitudes, is rejected and pushed into the unconscious. Repressed material gathers strength as the ideas try to be made known, for they are unrecognized aspects of one's unique personality. The self-regulating activities of the psyche strive toward wholeness, pressing for an expansion of consciousness, enabling both dark and light facets of the personality to be known and contained.

Depression is usually a sign that too much energy is having to flow inward, in order to keep repressed unconscious elements from being admitted into consciousness. Until these repressed elements can be acknowledged and accepted (that is, integrated), the neurotic condition will persist.

I talked with Leila about Jung's belief that individuation seeks wholeness, not perfection. The state of perfect piety, Leila's goal for herself, did not include recognition of repressed factors. This, in turn, led to the one-sidedness which gave rise to her depression.

As I listened to Leila's history, present situation and hopes for the future, I also attended to what was *not* being said, what was being excluded. I did not find much that included a healthy attitude toward her feminine nature, though she stated she wanted to do some body work. She was not well grounded in matter or reality and chose the comfort of idealism. Her physical symptoms of anorexia pointed to the literal starvation of the body, which suggested also the starvation of her sexuality. Eroticism and feminine self-confidence were alien to her conscious image of herself.

Although she seemed to have been long asleep, unconscious of herself as an individual, I sensed a deep yearning within. I thought she might have the capacity to look into the recesses of herself. Evidently she had more life to explore than the fragile, constricting, comely yet pious mask with which she identified.

If we were being called to gently open the door to the unknown aspects of Leila's personality, the essential first step would be to ground her disengaged ethereal spirit in the physical human body.

Leila

For the past twelve years I have lived with the fervent desire to tell the story of the unfolding of my womanhood. This process began when I entered analysis at the age of fifty. Until then, I had understood my inner life to be my conscious feelings, thoughts and prayers. I had no understanding of the nightly dramas in my dreams. As I began to recognize their implications, my awareness gradually changed.

Beginning to piece together the story, I realized that my idea of how it had come about was vague. I turned to my journal. Though I was impatient with the hours required to cull through the detailed accounts of my daily activities, endless turmoil and questions, excitement spurred me on. Bit by bit, from within the chaos, the thread of the mystery revealed itself.

Despite the generous hint from nature—each of us coming into and leaving the world alone—I had tried to escape the responsibility of my individuality. I existed on the surface, without discerning the depth of spirituality inherent in womanhood. I have never found a precise definition of spirit, but I can report my experiences and how I learned that my sexuality and spirituality are not the separate creatures I had made of them.

It was overwhelming to fathom that my inner narrative, intensely felt yet invisible to others, was the guiding influence in my external life. The encounters with my unconscious defy reason, though I know them to be real and have worked hard to find my own way of living them. These years have been difficult. Nancy served as my touchstone of sanity, while at the same time inviting me to open myself to irrational psychic factors. She constantly encouraged me to see what the next dreams would say, and I despaired when they prompted further questions. At this, she would reply, "We can only wait and see."

I write of my story, but it surely belongs as much to the dark-haired woman in my dreams. She and Nancy and I all struggled together. About a year into analysis, I glanced toward Nancy's lap at the folder containing my dreams. "You're holding my soul," I blurted out, and she nodded. This was my first glimpse of the depth of our venture.

The dark-haired woman has radically changed my attitudes. She awakened me to the innermost recesses of my femininity and showed me the beauty of my body and of intimacy. Our relationship has not been comfortable because I had to amend beliefs originally held as absolutes, teachings never doubted. More often than not I have wanted to evade her message, yet I have grown to trust her, enigma that she is, and perhaps may always be.

I remember well the September morning that my psychological journey began. I swallowed two Tranxene and a glass of wine to numb my nerves before boarding the plane to Alabama. In the motel I stretched across the bed to rest and slept past my four o'clock appointment. Distressed, I phoned and was surprised at the analyst's generosity in inviting me to come on to her office. When she opened the door I was immediately drawn to her and wished that I could be more like her. Yet, wanting to confirm her worth as a Christian, I scanned her tabletops and shelves for Bibles or devotional books. I spotted nothing and was too shy to inquire. Seated stiffly across from her, I poured out the details of my background.

I was born in 1937 in a small southern American town where my mother lived her entire life, enjoying the prestige of a highly respected family. There was enough money, and more still after she married, though the importance of this was denied, prominence in the community being of greater value. My father came from a neighboring city. A sports hero, he began his professional life in my mother's town and gained a widespread reputation as an honest Christian. I was the younger of two daughters, and we were constantly reminded that we were "well-born," which remained undefined beyond the intimation of superiority.

My hair was blonde, my eyes blue-green, and I was often described as a beautiful little girl. I became proud of this prettiness that brought me attention, and when growing gangly, tried to appear dainty. I adored hearing, "Look at Leila. Acting like the angel she is. Come here, darling." Exemplary as the sweet submissive child, my politeness and gentle manner were so praised by others that they became the whole basis for my sense of worth, to be maintained at all costs.

Typical of most southern females of my generation, I was trained to be always ladylike. My maternal grandmother lived with us until her death when I was fourteen, and she helped school me in the manifold commandments of ladyhood. I admired her regal figure and obeyed her dictates, hoping to be just such a great lady some day.

At the age of seven, I wore a long white costume as the Queen of Spring in the school play. I was taught to wear a robe over my pajamas and clean slippers. Displaying my toes, unless on the beach, was not proper; only common people did that. A little lady sat up straight with her knees and ankles pressed together, her skirt pulled down. She washed her face and hands and combed her hair when it was time for her daddy to come home. A little lady modulated her voice, laughing softly and never yelling.

At twelve, I was confirmed by the bishop of the Episcopal church with the laying on of hands. Riding to the service, my mother reminded me to keep my back straight and to stay attentive to my appearance. In a white eyelet dress, I knelt at the altar with pretended piety, remembering to turn my pretty profile toward the congregation. I was taught that a young lady wore a hat and white gloves to church. A young lady did not wear shorts when the minister visited. A young lady smiled brightly and spoke to everyone, her social equal or not.

When I reached menarche earlier than my friends, my mother directed me to hide the fact. Packing my bag for slumber parties, she concealed the sanitary napkins at the bottom. My one pursuit was to stay fresh and clean, otherwise never to think about or touch my body. It was dismissed as shameful.

At fifteen, having been elected Queen of the May by my classmates, I paused at the rear of the auditorium in a long white organdy gown. All eyes turned toward me, and I basked in their admiration as a wreath of white flowers was placed on my head. I was taught that a young lady avoids talking about herself, remaining modest at all times. A young lady wears a girdle under a tight skirt. A young lady does not let a boy kiss her.

At nineteen, in a long net gown, its whiteness broken by the red ro-
ses in my bouquet, I was a debutante. Appearing at my father's side, I
delighted in the guests' admiring glances. Though preoccupied with
obeying my mother's directions to keep my back straight and hair in
place, I felt special dancing in his arms.

Remembering all of this, I wept openly as I relived for Nancy the
feeling of my mother's hand on my back, nudging me forward. Her
urgent instructions had pestered me for decades: "Just smile and be
sweet and natural and you'll be fine." I now knew that I was anything
but fine.

Memories flooded me, and during the following analytic sessions I
continued my outpouring. When I fell in love in college, having been
taught that sex before marriage was immoral, I fought my desire. My
parents did not approve of the young man, but he was socially
prominent and my mother dictated my letters to ensure that he was
kept on the hook. After two years of happiness, one evening in his car,
parked outside my dormitory, he pulled away from a kiss. With tears,
he said that it was over because somehow he knew that I could not
give him what he needed. Devastated, I pined for months before con-
cluding that my mother had been right—he would never amount to
much.

To please my mother and achieve acceptance from others was all-
important. Frantic grooming usurped my energy, and years later I
realized that adorning my flesh to charm males, then turning away,
had caused me great harm. I did not detect my falseness, unaware
that the need to control my body expressed my hatred of it and that,
in effect, I was discarding myself.

At twenty-three, again in love, I glided down the aisle in my
mother's white silk wedding dress. She had often said, "My fortune
has been made, but yours . . ." This meant that she was securely mar-
ried, but I was at the early stages of securing my own. My sole respon-
sibility was to grip the arm of my husband. That night I wore a filmy
white gown with the matching peignoir tied beneath my chin. Kneel-
ing beside the bed, I pretended to pray while mentally checking my-

self to make sure I looked pure and lovely. I wanted to give myself to him, yet once under the covers, my desire evaporated. He was gentle, and I clenched my teeth to let happen what I had saved myself for. I feared losing him if I did not.

Into my married years I carried an image of myself as the delicate lady, at all times genteel. Psychologically, I still wore white.

I assumed someone would always take care of me. My parents could be relied on, and I had married a stable professional man. My father had instructed me to leave the Episcopal church for my husband's denomination, and shortly after the wedding, with characteristic submission, I obeyed. The social aspects attracted me, and I imitated the women I regarded as spiritual. In doing so, I was accepted. My mother directed me to use the time left from family to volunteer in my congregation, ever cautious against detracting from the men as leaders. I equated service with religious development and remained as cut off from my spiritual nature as from my physical.

I enrolled in numerous courses to learn to be a good Christian wife and continued to endure sex as duty. By seeking enlightenment from religion I believed that I was moving out on my own. I did not understand that I had substituted one authority for another, never making the effort to think for myself.

I again sobbed as I told Nancy about not being able to have children. For years I had experienced severe menstrual cramps, which after marriage was diagnosed as endometriosis. Even with fertility treatments, I did not become pregnant. Looking back, I acknowledged that this was a major indication of my negative attitude toward my femininity, but at the time I accepted the medical explanation that physical problems, which could not be overcome, were to blame.

After four years of bitter disappointment my husband and I adopted a baby boy. Lifting him into my arms, I felt that I finally belonged. Triumphantly, I pushed the stroller of this handsome blond nine-month-old boy in his freshly polished white shoes. I had a reason to live. During the following years we adopted two more beautiful babies, both girls, and I fit the pattern of what I thought a woman, as mother, should be. The adoption bureau emphasized honesty, and from their earliest days I cooed to "my precious adopted babies." Nevertheless, when pushing them in a swing on the playground or in a cart in the grocery store I pretended to be their birth mother.

I had qualms about my situation. A sense of dread pervaded each day, and any positive feelings about myself were soon obliterated. Knowing no alternative, I kept busy with daily "things-to-do" lists which I followed to the letter. The monthly cramps became unbearable, and a total hysterectomy was performed in an attempt to improve my quality of life. I never associated my diseased organs with my dis-ease about being a woman.

In my forties, my desperation mounted. Something within me was demanding to break loose, and I was terrified of what it might be. I held on tightly to my beliefs about myself, particularly to the notion of my lady-being. If I had given in to the dark doubts for even an instant, my world would have crumbled. Gritting my teeth, I maintained life as it had been in order to cover my despair, barely able to hide the gnawing at my insides. My pretenses drained my vitality.

As I told Nancy, tears constantly threatened as I strained to fulfill my obligations in the church and Junior League. I existed from party to party, wanting an occasion to report to my mother so I could bask in her approval, then finding myself with nothing to hold on to for security until the next event. Tending to my family became increasingly difficult. My older daughter was maturing, and I rejected her as a bad girl who required much correction. I had no idea at the time that I was reacting to the despised and neglected part of myself instead of to the beautiful young woman she was becoming..

My husband suggested a psychiatrist. Afraid of the disgrace if others learned that I was not all I had so skillfully feigned, I refused and doubled my efforts to keep the house perfectly clean, the meals perfectly delicious and healthy, our outings pleasing to everyone. Perfectionism became my shield against the pain of being human.

Finally, when the children were seventeen, fourteen and eleven, I began to consider suicide. No longer able to restrain the panic, I im-

plored my husband to call the psychiatrist. Though I viewed this as my lowest moment, it was actually the turning point.

I began treatment twice a week. The doctor prescribed medication to help me manage my depression and anxiety. I was surprised when she listened and evaluated what I had to say rather than patronizing me as the crazy nobody I judged myself to be. Her nurturing sustained me. During seven years of therapy, with the help of my husband, children and friends, I was able to carry on and gain some understanding of my illness.

Looking to the church for comfort and missing the Eucharist, I left my husband's denomination to join a small Episcopal congregation in the midst of charismatic renewal. The people were cordial, and I felt genuine while weeping at the altar. I sought healing through the laying on of hands and became convinced that faith in God the Father, and Jesus the Christ, would bring about my complete recovery from depression. I tried to be thankful in all things, and each morning wrote in my journal: "This is the day the Lord has made. I will rejoice and be glad in it." I addressed Abba-Daddy, pleading with him to remove my suffering. I more or less dismissed the symptoms of anorexia, measuring my well-being by the number on the bathroom scales and declaring my faith in an all-powerful, all-loving deity. I read Dietrich Bonhoeffer and heeded his advice to pray on scripture passages to avoid becoming a victim of my own emptiness. I soaked myself in prayer, making the rounds of the Bible studies and worship groups in various churches.

As messy as this was, it was an important step. Revealing my hurt compelled me to communicate less superficially. It was freeing to refuse social invitations with the answer that I was too depressed to be in a crowd, instead of the usual white lie. I soon went overboard and began to proclaim my misery to anyone who would listen. I felt that I was cutting into my false front, yet living out of my emotions was in fact a reaction to my parents' denial of theirs.

Trembling, I told Nancy that as a teenager I had eagerly confessed to my daddy that I knew I had been born to be one with God. He *chastised me for confusing feelings with faith, explaining that they were fickle and not to be trusted. Seeing myself as foolish, I quieted and learned to keep them to myself.*

In the course of working with the psychiatrist, I sold or gave away the furniture and silver received from my parents—beloved pieces my mother had urged me never to let out of the family. This was the first time I dared to go against her mandates.

Toward the end of my therapy, the psychiatrist suggested that I seek further help from a Jungian analyst and referred me to Nancy. Several weeks passed before I called her. Not only did I hate leaving the doctor I had come to depend on, but both my husband and our marriage counselor, an Episcopal priest, opposed it, concerned about my bewitchment with psychology.

At last, I wrote out every word I planned to say, and taking three big breaths I punched in Nancy's Birmingham number. I requested body work, adding that with therapy I was functioning fairly well and maybe a few sessions would suffice. She agreed to see me, stating that we would use my unconscious material because that was what she did, and asked me to bring my dreams.

Having been taught to ignore what came in the night, my anxiety escalated. My mother had stopped me from sharing them with her by scolding, "Nothing is more boring. And besides, that kind of talk makes you sound nutty." Was I indeed crazy?

At our first meeting, after a lengthy description of myself, I asked Nancy about "the feminine." (Smugly, I presumed that I had developed it, my concept being limited to the sentiment of the old song: "The girl that I marry will have to be / as soft and as sweet as a melody . . .") In her relaxed manner, she explained that it didn't exist without the body. She stressed the necessity of my commitment to analysis and the certainty of both tedium and fear. She assured me that I had within what I needed, and I sensed her support. Despite much foreboding, as I left our initial four sessions, I was relieved that an analyst was going to take a look at my dreams.

On the plane home I listed her suggestions:

1. Record my dreams and thoughts and feelings. Mail dreams a week before our next meeting.

2. Look at my nude body in the mirror.

3. Rub it with oil.

4. Write about it.

5. Experiment with various fabrics.

Perceiving these as assignments that I could not summon the energy to complete, I tapped the window glass while watching the clouds and whispered Nancy's parting words: "The wind won't always be at your back." I was afraid I wasn't going to make it, though I couldn't begin to define "it."

My psychiatrist asked about Nancy. I answered that I had been comfortable talking to her and considered her thoughtful, adding that she seemed rather common. Immediately appalled to hear myself use an adjective which implied everything I had been schooled to avoid, I reached for another to portray the person on whom I was relying. None came, and "common" returned whenever I pictured her. As vague as my comprehension was, I perceived in her a quality for which I lacked the vocabulary—a woman all together, common yet not common. Somehow she was both.

2
The Dark-Haired Woman and the Rat

I am sitting on a single bed at a beach house. A dark-haired lady is beside me. I see a movement under the rug, than a second movement, then a third. A rat emerges from the other side of the bed. I am afraid and scream. A rat pounces on me, and I scream to the dark-haired woman to get it off me. She stands and just stares at me for a long time, then finally beats the rat away with a pillow. I am panic stricken.

The beach house, in Leila's association, was the place where she spent summers as a child and adolescent. She recognized the single bed as hers. Summer at the beach was not the fun-filled vacation one might imagine. Whereas there were fewer constraints regarding dress and manners, other restrictions hampered the child's natural curiosity, her sense of play and imagination. She was not allowed to enter the ankle-deep water alone nor roam the beach without being under someone's watchful eye. Activities promoting a sense of confidence or of one's direction in self-development were overshadowed by the constant reminder of the need for someone to guide or protect her.

The dream image of sitting on the side of the bed seems to indicate she was awakening from a long sleep. As mentioned earlier, we find a similar theme, an archetypal pattern, in "Sleeping Beauty." In that fairy tale the princess, on her fifteenth birthday, falls into a sleep of a hundred years because of the curse of the uninvited fairy godmother. Physiologically as well as psychologically, this is the age when a young girl is developing into womanhood and her sexuality is awakened. If she "falls asleep," that is, stays unconscious, her psychic rite of passage into womanhood can never occur. Psychologically, she will remain a maiden.

At the time Leila entered adolescence, young girls were often oppressed by old wives' tales and cultural restrictions. Menstruation was commonly referred to as "the curse," implying something evil about monthly bleeding and the female body. Leila's story told of many other curses, all stemming from the fact that sex or sexual feelings were disgusting and cheapened a "proper woman." Another curse that shaped Leila's attitudes was that her body was to be beautiful only for the purpose of attracting a "good" man who would adore and take care of her. That her body was a vessel for love and pleasure was not even a distant thought.

The "wicked godmothers" in our culture are those women who keep these viewpoints alive, casting a spell on their daughters through generations. Fortunately, women in most parts of the Western world are awakening to the fact that these attitudes, which prevailed during the time and place of Leila's upbringing, are erroneous and unhealthy. In order not to deal with the conflict between her natural desires and parental or cultural dictates, Leila, like Sleeping Beauty, fell asleep, thus remaining psychologically in a state of maidenhood. The injunctions against her sexual nature may be seen as the building blocks of her neurosis. Her basic instinctual nature was repressed—split off and sealed away.

Now the dream tells us that something dark and loathsome is emerging from under the rug. Rats are generally associated with something living in dank, filthy places. A creature despised, it cannot be ignored because of its characteristic gnawing. It spreads disease, scurrying around in the night, emerging only for frightening glimpses. The rat is an animal associated with witches, and thus is seen as a harbinger of evil. This dream image presents a graphic picture of Leila's unconscious attitude toward her body and her sexuality, a picture clearer than her conscious words would have expressed.

I found this dream informative and promising in several ways, even though Leila viewed it with horror. First, the rat was only beneath a thin surface, the rug; it was not deep in the bowels of a sewer, for instance. The image was more accessible to consciousness and could be worked with without too much difficulty. An aspect of life which is split off, such as that which the rat symbolizes, demands attention. It pounces on the dreamer!—which is often how it feels when repressed unconscious material breaks through to consciousness. This dream image jars her to wakefulness. Look! Be aware! That is its message.

Leila noted that she felt panic stricken in the dream and also when telling it to me. "Panic" is a word derived from Pan, the phallic god associated with untamed, instinctual sexuality. Something was trying to enter consciousness in order to redeem that which had been repressed for so long.

Secondly, a woman who in reality is unknown emerges in the dream as an ally. When writing down the dream, Leila first calls her a dark-haired *lady,* but when she comes to her aid she is referred to as a dark-haired woman. The distinction between lady and woman is clear, a distinction Leila had difficulty making other than that women are common and a lady is sophisticated. Here it was the woman, not the lady, who was unafraid of the rat and could deal with what it symbolized. The dark-haired woman, opposite to Leila's blondness, is a shadow aspect of her personality. In Jungian terms, the shadow is a personification of repressed contents that are incompatible with one's image of oneself—attitudes, values and appearance. The shadow can also be viewed as unlived life.

This was the first dream Leila brought to analysis. One's initial dream usually indicates the main focus of the analysis. To me, this dream underscored the need to bring to consciousness shadow material containing both the dark aspects of Leila's repressed sexuality and the light aspects of the dark-haired woman who would help her.

Leila

Having trouble coping with daily activities and in concentrating, but determined to work hard in analysis, I diligently recorded my dreams. Yet when not actually talking with Nancy I remained detached from the images, continuing to live very much on the surface. Despite being nearly overwhelmed by panic, I pressed blindly ahead, thinking that to survive I had to push myself without mercy. I had absolutely no idea that I could make choices in my own way, with individual timing. I thought my ego was the instrument for healing, and if I developed it everything would fall into place. I did not understand that the images themselves contained the seeds I needed and that the dark-haired woman could help.

Yet I was aware that my personality was governed by excessive "shoulds," and wanted more than anything to rid myself of them. I was willing to work toward this end, to the exclusion of almost all else. Since my breakdown, to endure anxiety I walked a couple of miles most days. I remembered my mother pointing to a neighbor, saying, "That nutty woman walks and walks. Isn't she pitiful?" Now, circling block after block, I pictured people staring from windows to spew just such judgments about me.

Coming in from my trek one morning, I resolved to complete the assignment to view my body. I went straight to the bedroom. While stripping, my uneasiness mounted, and I closed my eyes as I approached the full-length mirror in the corner. I could not look. Pacing around the room and into the hall, weeping with frustration, I prayed for forgiveness for my no-good self. Tasting the salt on my lips, I made a pact with myself, promising that when my tears hit my stomach I would peek. A starving female, reminding me of the photographs of Auschwitz, stared out at me. Unable to bear the sight, I threw on my clothes.

Two weeks later I again stood before the mirror. Yes, I belonged in a coffin. I did, however, admire my breasts. In subsequent encounters, I watched my hands apply lotion to my legs and arms, then to my breasts and feet. I accepted that I had to stroke my body to animate it, as if it were an infant requiring touch in order not to perish.

At supper one evening I remarked to my husband that I was glad we had sidewalks in our part of town because I could stroll and usually bump into someone to chat with.

"Lots of idle ladies around," he commented.

I was crushed that he saw me like this, yet I, too, believed myself to be nothing but a pampered, insignificant female. To prove my worth, I broadened my volunteer endeavors.

3
Too Many Layers

I am in a hospital room. Mother is sitting on the bed watching me dress. She tells me to put on more and more clothes. First a white blouse, then a red blouse, then a red dress over that, then a black one and black beads. She criticizes every piece and I am miserable. I see a dresser and rush over to plunder the drawers. Disheveled pieces of old clothing fill each one, but I know they are her clothes and I am going to be all right.

The setting of this dream in a hospital room indicates that there is an illness, yet it also implies a promise, for a hospital room is a place where healing may begin. It is unclear who is the patient—mother or daughter, or both. Their diagnosis may be thought of as the same, though perhaps in different degree. As we have seen from Leila's history, her mother's illness is infectious. The disease, that of repressing one's true feminine nature, is no less contagious and deadly to soul and body than was the Great Plague of the thirteenth century, spread by rats.

The focus of the dream is clothes of all descriptions. Mother instructs the dreamer in what she must wear, how she must appear to others. Mother demands that her daughter's image mirror her own. There is no recognition that mother and daughter are separate individuals. We realize in the beginning of the dream that Leila has no sense of self, no ego that defines who she may be. The hospital scene was not unlike Leila's reality, for, as she explained, her mother chose the clothes she would wear and what was considered appropriate for every occasion. There was rarely a time when she had the opportunity to exercise her own will in such matters.

Clothes are a symbol of the persona, our public personality. The word "persona" comes from the Greek word for mask; it is the "face" one wears in social situations. It is a necessary protection that defends our most vulnerable feelings from the barbs of everyday life. It eases our way through the trials of simply living. The danger comes when one identifies with the persona. The mask becomes stuck, so to speak, and there is no face, no vital person behind it. We simply become the role we are assigned, or have chosen, to play—the professor, the cleric, the executive, the wife—and are cut off from the flow of life's vital forces from within.

The white costumes of pivotal celebrations in Leila's developing years symbolized the persona with which she identified. Purity, Innocence, Beauty, Grace—these were the qualities she presented to others, yet the naked truth underneath was symbolized by the dark-haired woman and the rat.

In the dream there are layers and layers of persona issues which mother has commanded her daughter to wear, a shade or style for every occasion. Some are hidden away, out of sight, but are readily available as the occasion requires. All is a mess and belongs to Mother, a sick persona where the mask is rigidly stuck. Leila finds her voice at the end of the dream, in a personality differentiated from her mother. Consciously realizing how much of her mother's beliefs and values she has unconsciously "worn," Leila now becomes aware that she had no idea who she is under all those layers.

How to find the way to change these attitudes was another matter and a difficult one. But in this liminal place, jarring reality has become clear: I am not who I thought I was, but I know not who I am. It is a necessary time of dissolution of old psychic structures, without hope for, or awareness of, what new structures may develop. One feels, as did Leila, a sense of chaos and despair.

Leila

The parade in white through my formative years had been choreographed by my mother, and most of my dreams took me back to my childhood home. It was becoming increasingly clear to me that her influence remained constant in everything I thought about myself. Lacking the authenticity to be myself, like a rebellious teenager I now often refused to respond to social invitations. I needed to do this in order to see that the world would not come to an end as a consequence, for my mother had radiated a sense of impending disaster when I begged not to attend such functions. This dark anxiety persisted into my adult life. Regardless of the social repercussions, I had to find something with more meaning than my automatic reactions.

I was still stuck in acting out what she had wanted, and when I stopped I discovered I did not know where I wanted to go or what I wanted to say. In fact, I had no idea what was truly important to me.

Back during my breakdown, I came up against my parents' distrust of psychiatry. A friend of the family was being treated, and my mother repeatedly said, "She's acting nutty, going away by herself. That's what that psychiatrist is doing to her." She stated that I should not hurt my husband and children by seeking help and urged me to consider our standing in the community. The message that we were too well-born for mental illness was understood. (I later learned that an uncle's suicide and a great-aunt's psychosis had been kept a secret.)

My psychiatrist advised me to stop communicating with my mother, in order to lessen the threat of her judgments. Though a life-saving decision at the time, family members chided me for cruelty and people in my church warned that my unwillingness to forgive blocked the blessings of the holy spirit. All of this engendered terrific guilt.

As in the dream, so in reality I literally struggled with my clothes, spending hours sorting through them, then shopping and often returning my purchases because they no longer seemed to suit me. Prim necklines and pastel colors, especially pink, which were for little girls, had to go. Fighting guilt, I tossed many of my things into the trash. Having found the styles I would not choose, I wasn't sure which I would, though I was particularly attracted to the color purple. (My mother had disliked it, thinking it common, and had forbidden me to wear it.) As the months wore on I learned to recognize the clothes symbolic of the persona she had demanded of me. I would tell myself, again and again: "No, these are my mother's. I will not wear them."

Active Imagination: Princess No-Face

Shortly after I began analysis my mother was hospitalized. One after-noon while I sat in her room, she reminisced about her childhood. Nose tilted upward, she announced that her father had thought she was perfect, and if he walked in that very minute nothing would have changed. I'd often heard this tale, and when she waved toward the door had always expected my grandfather to enter.

While politely listening, like a shock from I know not where, "princess" occurred to me. The following week, during my plane trip to Birmingham, I relived the scene and, stung by the revelation, wept. Wiping my eyes before my seat-mates noticed, I wrote a story about myself. The final refrain showed me sitting in my garden, sadder than ever, sighing:

> *I am Princess No-Face.*
> *Queen Mother said never frown, Face.*
> *Queen said always smile, Face.*
> *King said never cry, Face.*
> *Where is my face?*
> *Where, oh where, is my face?*

During the ensuing weeks I pored over the words. Much of my hopelessness coursed through this melancholy song. With no face, the person I had become had no voice either, no eyes to see for herself or ears to hear for herself. My life thus far had no individuality. This was a truth I could no longer deny.

Later, in understanding that my mother's illness had risen partly from her need to be perfect in her father's eyes, I saw that I was no different, except I had wanted to be perfect for her.

Nancy repeatedly challenged me to consider how I was serving the princess part of myself, but in my despair and confusion at letting her go, I could verbalize very little.

*

There are times when images or words stressing a mental attitude break through into consciousness and we are visibly shaken. We feel hounded by strong emotion. Attending to these images is as important as listening to our dreams for they all arise from our unconscious. We work with them by collecting our associations to them, by active imagination, and by keeping them in our mind's eye so that the image *and* emotion continue to be wrestled with, rather than repressed again. Leila made a "word picture" by writing a story of the princess and the life she lived.

The image of, and interaction with, Princess No-Face was very stressful, but it allowed a change in Leila's understanding. Previously, she had identified with the helpless fairy-tale princess who awaits a prince to rescue her. Leila knew no other model. In that role, she remained emotionally immature, without the depth needed to reflect on her individuality. In that undifferentiated space, she knew herself only as defined by others, usually men. The face she turned to the world had no distinctive features. Psychologically she could never become a queen, that is, the dominant ruler of her feminine nature. Yet, without this ruling principle, relatedness to self and others is invariably ineffectual.

4
The Hollow-Shell Woman

A human form, completely covered with a sheet, is on a bed. I watch it move a little. Enraged, I climb on top of it and attack to kill. I must kill it. I begin strangling this form, and the sheet slides off. I see a white woman, a pasty white blonde china-like doll with a red circle painted on each cheek. So like a china doll, but real. She is naked. I can feel her flesh as I try to strangle her. She crumbles in my hands—she was a shell! I can see through holes where her eyes were that she is totally empty. She has no insides. (My husband wakens me because the doll-woman and I are screaming.)

The image of the hollow-shell woman resembles the grotesque image in an earlier dream of a woman kept alive, yet lifeless, in a laboratory flask: blonde hair, painted cheeks and bloodless complexion. The difference, however, is that the laboratory woman, like a blown-up doll, is inflated in an artificial way, while the woman under the sheet is now recognized as hollow, only a shell of superficiality. Still, she remains alive and is capable of movement.

Like ghosts from our past, images symbolizing the character of a worn-out persona haunt us in dreams. Leila did not wish to identify with the little princess doll, as she had once envisioned herself, but the attitudes of a lifetime are slow to die. The coy yet demanding princess remains an aspect of Leila's personality. Consciously knowing how destructive this can be, of course she wants to be rid of it.

Dreams not only illustrate the psyche's search for balance, they also make us aware of the times when we regress into old patterns of behavior. Perhaps the day or even several days before this dream, Leila had resolved some conflict by resorting to old behavior, albeit unconsciously. The dream was registering this fact.

It is a frightening undertaking to remove the mask with which one

34

has become so identified, for we are indeed left with no face. Family and close friends are also bewildered when one's personality begins to change. Instead of agreeing submissively, Leila was starting to express her own opinions. "What's gotten into her?" they all thought. Leila sensed their disapproval and felt very lonely. How very easy it would be to return to old behaviors.

The path of individuation becomes more narrow and demanding as one progresses. Unrelentingly, the dream forces us to examine and reexamine ourselves.

Leila

With this dream, the images began to get through to me. For days the picture of the crumbling shell interrupted my thoughts, and my all-consuming hatred of it was difficult to put aside. I was indeed empty, covered over with an insipid mask. Realizing this was devastating. I could find no compassion for myself. Princess No-Face had brought me to this end, and I despised her little-girl-lost persona. I became desperate to rid myself of this hollowness.

Searching my journal, I found page after page of accusations against my husband. I blamed him because I was stuck in the role of supportive wife, required only to revel in his achievements. I was certain that if only he would change, things would be different for me. I never examined how unfair this attitude was.

I did not know what to do, for I could not stop denouncing him or being fake. Any comment that I was a good person brought up an entire assortment of unwanted pictures of my piety. Terrifically frustrated, I despaired, concealing my vulnerability by staying home as much as possible.

I've often considered how aptly this dream expressed the inner void I lived with and the false self I adopted to hide it. I truly wanted to murder her. Instead of blood, the waxiness of her doll-likeness soiled my hands. Somehow I had to free myself.

5
The Closet Child

I am a school teacher, cleaning and decorating the room for the year. I find that a child has been living in the closet. There is excrement, filth and food everywhere. A committee comes to inspect my schoolroom and walks away disgusted that I have allowed this to happen. They say the damage is beyond repair. I see a bed in the room and decide to get into it, but it too is dirty and full of food crumbs.

Once Leila could let go of her mask—her identity with the little princess—new images could emerge. (But such deeply rooted personalities are very difficult to be rid of—the Little Princess returns often.) The child living in filth and waste is the opposite of the snow-white princess. Recalling a previous dream where a wise voice stated that a child had been abandoned since the age of one, we now find the hidden child and bring it to the light of consciousness.

The child embodies potential life and the authenticity of innocence. Many powerful emotions had been shoved into a closet, or we could say repressed. The dream tells us of the consequence: the neglected child became dirty and dreadful. The closet child represents a life which is neglected and contaminated by its own waste. But within that image sleeps the archetype of the divine child which derives from the Self, symbol of wholeness.

As Leila and I spoke of this dream I explained that when an infant does not see her own delight reflected in her parents' eyes, the natural child is repressed at a very early age. The adaptive child, or we could say the false self, takes its place. In Leila's case this false self was molded into the Little Princess. She told of a time when as a child playing in a neighbor's tree-house, she had been "rescued" by her father, with the admonishment that she should never do that again for she could so easily be hurt. She never did play in that tree house again.

As with the constant guarding at the beach, as a child Leila received no message other than that she was a fragile being in a dangerous world, and could not take care of herself.

In this dream, Leila sees herself as a school teacher, endowed with the capabilities of a mentor and caretaker, tending to the long-ignored aspect of herself that has been living in the closet. And no less than the teacher, the dream ego now must grant nurturing and empathy to the closet child. So too, Leila must attend to the flood of emotions which follow discovery of that abandoned aspect of herself.

The child represents not only new life but also a new imaginative force that produces a wellspring of curiosity and creativity if it is lovingly tended. The committee in the dream evaluates classroom conditions, as school review committees do, noting beneficial aspects but also pinpointing the source of negligence. This committee corresponds to that part of the psyche that is self-regulating, aimed at balancing psychic processes so that one may journey toward wholeness. The dream committee finds extreme neglect of all that is embodied by the image of a child. Although its judgment is harsh, it reflects the no-nonsense tone that is needed in this situation. Going to bed and pulling the covers over one's head is not a healthy option, as the dirty cot in the closet reveals. The task of loving what appears to be unlovable is difficult because it is ego consciousness that must do it—the same ego that originally repressed those characteristics.

As with the loathsome rat under the rug, the closet child is an image not to turn away from, however painful. Imagining the feelings of the closet child—loneliness, terror, hunger for love—keeps one emotionally in touch with that neglected, locked-up aspect of oneself that is potentially so vital.

Leila
For several sessions Nancy and I discussed this dream at length, then I promptly dismissed the child in the closet. Having hoped for some-one more exciting and easier to deal with to appear in my dreams, I did not bother with her. Though Nancy referred to her throughout the

ensuing weeks, she did not seem real to me.

Finally I had a change of heart. I was feeling particularly upset and vulnerable, and Nancy poured us a cup of tea from a plump blue china pot. I sensed that she was having a tea party with this closet child, perhaps about five years old. Deeply impressed with her interest, I too decided to take her seriously.

One morning when bending to make my bed, I noticed the door to the closet standing open. As I shut it, I recalled my grandmother's words: "Nothing betrays an otherwise perfect room like a gaping closet." Suddenly the truth came: we had indeed imprisoned my spontaneous child-self. My hand on the knob, wanting to reopen it, I hesitated, and my need for order won. How would I ever overcome my compulsion for neatness, which bordered on an obsession, and allow this little girl to make a mess?

Doubting that I could, nevertheless each night I dated the pad on my bedside table, ready to receive my dreams, and frequently drifted to sleep while thinking of this child. Though I did not fully grasp what was happening, the tablet was in essence the door through which I entered the world where she was hidden and invited her out.

I really wanted to help her, but having identified some of the controlling facets of the mothering I'd had and that I, in turn, had given my three children, I questioned my ability to communicate positively with this image. Nancy emphasized that my awareness made the difference, but I felt unable to hold her close, and my aspiration to nurture often evaporated. Knowledge of my barren state, the empty shell of a woman in the previous dream, brought recurring depression. What proved stronger than this was my realization that no one else on earth could help this child. I was her only hope. Over the months she made herself tangible in myriad ways.

Undressing for bed one evening, tired of my apparently unending conflict, I whispered to the mirror, "I can't do it." From within came, "Mommy, mommy. I'm just a tiny girl." I knew the cry to be from my closet child. She needed to weep and she had no ears but mine to hear her. My compassion grew. Excited about getting to know her, I called her Ann, the middle name I had never used and which now seemed fitting for a life I had never lived.

I doubled my attempts to connect with her, and in place of the familiar refrain, ". . . this I know, for the Bible tells me so," I sang, "This child I know, for my dreams tell me so." Yet, as the days passed, she constantly slipped away from me.

One morning after showering I clutched a pillow to my chest and ran to an empty closet in the attic. My heart skipped as I shut the door. Lowering myself to the floor, hating the darkness, I hugged my knees and buried my face in the pillow. The church bells from the next block tolled ten, followed by a car horn, then the muffled comments of passersby. I raised my head to see a line of light below the door and placed my mouth there to breathe. Stroking my skin, I found it tender to my fingers and my body ached with sorrow. "Ann, how have you endured these endless years?" I wept.

My visit in the closet, even for this short period, made her like flesh and blood to me. Guilt stricken, I realized that I had abandoned her for forty-five years, and I marveled at her survival. (As far back as memory could take me, I had been afraid of the dark. Considering this immature, I kept it a secret. In my fifties, I still could not talk myself out of it. Over the following years this fear, which had been Ann's, disappeared.) I sang a lullaby and patted my own arms and cheeks, trusting that Ann would be soothed. I composed stanzas for her and intoned them like a spiritual: "Oh, little closet child, poor little closet girl, been in the dark so long, so long. Come out, closet one, your mourning time is done . . ." As I walked along the rows of supplies in the supermarket or made coffee or waited at a stoplight, I hummed my spiritual under my breath. She was comforted, as was I.

Relating to both Princess No-Face and Ann, I was repeatedly confused about which emotion belonged to whom. Whenever I felt I had no right to enjoy or even no right to be, I usually mistook it for the whining of the princess. Gradually I recognized it as Ann's cry for love. Conversely, though I had thought that it was the closet child spilling her anguish to my husband, ruining our marriage, gradually

I came to see that these irruptions were the princess's tantrums.

As I sorted things out, I was often disoriented, feeling crazy much of the time. Nancy assured me that this very craziness made me genuine. It took me many years to concur because of my overwhelming fear of losing control. Later I appreciated that having been overly restrained, this little child-in-me tumbled out of the closet in chaotic, unadapted fashion. Frightening as this was, my struggle to listen to her was teaching me to heed the neglected parts of my personality.

One afternoon as I sat sobbing, it occurred to me that the tears were Ann's. On impulse, I washed my face and drove to buy her a gift. Walking up and down the aisles of a large toy store, I reached for a soft, blue-eyed baby doll with blonde hair. Feeling exposed, I told the sales clerk that it was for my granddaughter (non-existent). Back home I held her to my cheek and rocked, then stood in front of the mirror. Who lived? The woman gazing back at me or the weeping child within? At this point I thought it had to be one or the other, not both.

By returning to the mirror again and again, I could at last envision Ann, though I was never certain of her age. At times she seemed more mature than at others. Staring into her eyes, I apologized for the years of deprivation. Sobered by my obligation to be her life-line, I attended her with a respect she'd never experienced.

In analysis I came to understand that my parents had wanted a princess. Being this for them brought me approval. It had become my security and I had chosen to sustain that easy life. By trusting the dream of the child abandoned in the closet I gradually became aware of that hidden aspect of myself. I had to make certain not to treat her like my mother had treated me, but to grant this natural child her say. Ever so slowly I comprehended that I was no longer the princess, yet who my authentic self might be I still did not know.

6
Leaving the Church

I leave my church and walk around the block. I discover five donkeys roaming the street. I am vaguely alarmed, mostly puzzled, and cross to the other side. A tiger comes after me, racing through the donkeys. I run up the front steps of a house, reach through many cobwebs and knock on the window for help. Two woman friends are in the kitchen. It seems a long time until they finally raise the window in answer to my screams. Then they only look at me. I urge them to call the police. One friend does this, and men appear with space-man type machines ejecting juices all over the place. I run from the juice. I see the tiger escape to the back of the house. I tell the men, but they never find it.

Thoughts of leaving the church were fearful to Leila for it was in this community, ironically, that she found acceptance and belonging because, as Leila said, she was "sick." As with any institution or organization, to be a member one adapts one's beliefs to collective patterns. There is no room for individuality except within the context of prescribed beliefs. Striving for psychic balance, this dream recalls the general attitudes about sex and specifically about feminine sexuality taught by her mother and underscored by Leila's religious beliefs. What were once accepted as absolute truths are dissolving, giving way to new images.

It is only when Leila, the dream ego, leaves the church (or what the church represented to her) to go out on the street, a place where common people gather, that other events can happen. And there marvelous things are indeed happening.

First she sees the donkeys. Animals in dreams often depict instinctive nature related to characteristic traits of the particular creature; the animal form connotes that the trait hasn't become "humanized" or conscious to the dreamer. The donkey or ass is frequently found in

41

Biblical passages as the royal mount of Christ, Solomon or Mary on her flight to Egypt. Also, it was through the donkey's mouth that God spoke to Balaam, so we could think of a religious symbol here except it was only when she left the church that the donkeys were first seen.

Other characteristics we associate with the donkey are that it is a beast of burden, a lowly animal, stubborn and dumb. These amplifications also did not seem applicable to this dream. I found other associations that better fit the context and Leila's psychological situation. Folklore maintains that the donkey is always in heat and thus is a symbol of a raw sexuality.

In alchemy, there is a figure of a three-headed ass termed *daemon triunus*, the chthonic Trinity, belonging to earth or matter. The donkeys, five of them, move without direction. The number five is symbolic of the pentagram of man, wholeness in a sense, with head and four limbs encircled (as portrayed in the familiar sketch by Leonardo da Vinci). It is as if the dream is completing or compensating for the "sexual black hole" in Leila's consciousness.

More explicitly, the ass is also the mount of Dionysus, the Greek god of irrational, instinctive nature. It symbolizes archetypal energy in direct opposition to the Apollonian stance of reason, order and control ingrained in educational, religious and governmental institutions. Dionysus embodies madness, intoxication, pandemonium, sexuality and ecstasy. This god is the creative spirit of art, science and love—the intoxication one feels in the heat of creativity, the moments in love when one surrenders to ecstasy.

The other animal racing through the streets is a tiger, long associated with the goddesses. The Egyptian goddess Hathor is often depicted in a feline form, while the cat was the companion to Artemis. The Nordic goddess Freya's chariot was drawn by two cats. We find in the tiger a relation to the divine feminine, raw and untamed. Once again, it is the mount of Dionysus, sent by Zeus to help him cross the Tigris. Yet as this image of instinctive feminine nature emerges— large, strong, quick and beautiful—and demands to be recognized, it causes great fear. And it should be noted how the image of the tiger, symbolizing much the same as the image of the rat, has changed from that of something emerging from darkness and filth to an image of beauty and majestic power. Unconscious contents have been somewhat modified by Leila's conscious acceptance of her body.

The dream ego seeks aid at a house where the women are caught in the web of domesticity, the very place Leila has excelled throughout her life. Cobwebs are spun by spiders in order to entrap their prey. Although intricate in design, as was Leila's social milieu, webs entangle and hinder movement. The dreamer can no longer find solace in this milieu; the role of model wife and mother, socially approved and religiously correct, is no longer a safe haven.

Instead of help from the police, the conscious element of rational law and order, alien space-type figures appear, men from another sphere—the remote inner space of the unconscious. We do not know if they are helpful or not, but with "juices" spewing out they appear potent. These juices are analogous to semen, the vital fluid necessary to create new life. Her fear in the dream also relates to the apprehension of male sexuality. Although Leila enlists the aid of these aliens (unknown factors from the unconscious) to find the tiger, they are unable to do so. I think that is appropriate at this time. There must be more conscious understanding of the vitality of her own feminine nature before masculine attributes from the unconscious can make a contribution to consciousness. Otherwise, the feminine principle could be overpowered. In outer reality as well as inner, a woman must appreciate her own feminine nature and gain a sense of ego strength in this identity lest it become vulnerable to definition or limitation by patriarchal dictates.

In Western culture chic magazines and other media have created the test-tube woman that appeared in Leila's earlier dream: a two-dimensional figure kept alive in the laboratory of the patriarchy's imagination. Leila must first meet this powerful tiger image eye-to-eye in order to earn a sense of feminine ego strength. The lysis of the dream suggests that the tiger is lost once again, and not without reason. A powerful aspect of feminine nature has been experienced by consciousness, but to integrate it into the total personality will take more time.

This dream reminds me of a passage from Jung. He writes,

> "Spirit" is one aspect, "Nature" another. "You may pitch Nature out with a fork, yet she'll always come back again," says the poet. Nature *must not* win the game, but she *cannot* lose. And whenever the conscious mind clings to hard and fast concepts and gets caught in its own rules and regulations . . . nature pops up with her inescapable demands. Nature is not matter only, she is also spirit. Were that not so, the only source of spirit would be human reason.[2]

Leila

At the time of this dream I was actually considering resigning from my church. Though never previously having put personal impulses before attendance, instead of Sunday clothes I now often slipped on jeans to drive to a private spot on the beach to write in my journal. In retrospect, I know that I was letting go of my need for those in authority to tell me how to live, but it did not feel freeing until much later. Leaving my safe, familiar church home was frightening, and I endured a great deal of conflict.

I was still drawn to the social activities of the church. Giving up the acceptance and fellowship of the women I regarded as spiritual was a wrenching experience, and I questioned if I could indeed choose loneliness. I knew I would also miss the beauty of the liturgy. Yet traditional interpretations of the Christian message no longer satisfied me. Worship was hollow, reminding me of the dream of a shell woman I wanted to murder. I mourned these losses, while beneath the grief lurked the impression that my dreams were somehow pushing me out the door.

Anger fueled my departure. I was as enraged at this institution as at my mother. I criticized it incessantly, irritated that others did not agree. I had always followed my mother's advice to use the energy

---

[2] "Paracelsus As a Spiritual Phenomenon," *Alchemical Studies,* CW 13, par. 229.

left over from family to volunteer in my congregation, ever cautious of detracting from the men as leaders. This service I had equated with religious development. I now faced many spare hours. Most of my family and friends were busy in their own denominations of one kind or another. Their reports of uplifting activities fanned my fury.

My biggest problem was that without parish activities there seemed to be no "me." I told myself this was ridiculous. Nevertheless it was a fact. Who was I without the blessing of the church? How could I tell?

And there was guilt—I heard it in my voice when I met my priest on the sidewalk and stumbled over words to explain my absence at worship. I was particularly uncomfortable when acquaintances I had not seen for a while asked which church I now attended. Dreading their disapproval, I usually laughed nervously as I admitted that there wasn't one. Most, thinking I would return when I was finished rebelling, did not take me seriously.

Solitary hours stretched ahead. I grappled with whether to yield or not until finally, wanting to take a stand, with trembling fingers I punched in the number of the church office to have my name erased. In the recesses of my heart I knew that I had to find my own way and my own truth.

I was regularly consumed with fresh regret for leaving. My parents' numerous religious exhortations came to mind. I held to my decision, beginning to discern that disobedience to their decrees was causing my remorse. I made only a few more visits to my congregation.

Often I rebuked myself for exaggerating my feeling of homelessness. After all, I had many material luxuries. But emotionally I was as out-in-the-cold as if I were huddled on the pavement. I struggled to overcome my fear of being left out and to turn inward to wrestle with my unknown side.

This brought me face to face with my dread of sex. It had been so intense that I had habitually plotted to be too busy or too weary or too sick. I had failed at receiving my husband, which I had been convinced was my obligation as a Christian wife. As I began to give up reacting to sex as duty, I yearned to experience physical passion and found myself again needing help.

My husband and I met with a sex therapist. Her personal warmth relaxed me, and it was not the clinical ordeal I had expected. As I listened to my husband I was amazed at the differences in our stories. His attitude toward the naturalness of his body and my shame about mine were extreme opposites. Though I still blamed him for my un-happiness, I began to understand that my injuries marked my starting point. My reproaches, both of myself and him, decreased. Hearing my background, he acknowledged my impasse and supported me.

Individual sessions with the therapist augmented the mirror work Nancy prompted me to continue. I spent hours there. The old warn-ings to be modest and not touch myself or allow others to do so kept ringing in my head. Recognizing on an ever-deepening level why I had rejected my body, I could begin to cooperate with it.

Emphasizing the sensual, the therapist gave us clear directions for exercises to be done at home. They proved to be as difficult as a for-eign language, yet expressing myself through my senses encouraged my imagination. My husband and I tried to lower our expectations. I was granted control of the assignments and stopped whenever I felt too anxious. This was often, since his masculinity was as fearful to me as the tiger and the men with their juices in the dream.

Progress was slow and defeat usually overwhelmed me. In the safety of the therapist's office I'd imagine the silk of my gown brush-ing my thighs and my fingers moistened with scented oil sliding down my husband's back, only to retreat in tears when I tried to implement my plans. But I persevered.

One morning I reached for the phone while making our bed with new black sheets that I thought were sexy. A friend invited me to a communion service that evening. Refusing, I stroked the sheet, pleased with my own undertaking. The sensuality exercises were be-coming my current form of prayer.

Yet my shame persisted, frequently paralyzing me. I gradually per-ceived that I had to trust my body itself, paying close attention to my reactions. For untold hours I studied each inch. I admired its graceful movements and tried to excuse its awkward ones. My physical self was the last place from which I anticipated reassurance, and using my time to make such observations went against what I thought I should be doing. As the weeks passed, something kept me at it.

Contrary to reason, the fear of carrying out the therapist's proposals escalated. It was as if in the midst of our lovemaking my closet child would wince, and I had to silently console her while opening sexually to my man. His masculinity continued to panic me, and this made little sense. Terrifically impatient, I berated myself: "Leila, can't you get it through your head that this is okay?" But it was my body that needed educating, not my head.

The knowledge that I couldn't give myself freely to my husband, that psychologically I was still my parents' little girl, was devastating. I so wanted to allow myself to be sexual instead of proper.

I envied the apparent ease that some women had with their bodies. On a whim I bought a large square of bright purple fabric. When preparing for our exercises, I disrobed and draped it round myself to dance for the mirror. I was becoming less reticent to view my nude self and more readily touched my skin.

My commitment to life had been based on a strict code of behavior. Now, with the many changes taking place, I was both apprehensive and intrigued that my "Ann" might develop values different from those I had learned all too well.

7
The Marriage Wheelchair

My husband and I are on a college campus. We are sitting in a wheelchair together. I want to get up and walk to the bus stop in the distance to wait for the next bust [sic], but I am afraid because it looks like rain.

When we find an intimate other in dreams, as we often do, it is problematic whether to take such images objectively—that is, as the real external person—or to look at them subjectively, as symbolic of one's inner man or woman (animus or anima), or as both. In this dream, because of the short duration of the analysis, I interpreted the husband objectively only, as her mate in outer life. The wheelchair presented a most comprehensive symbol of their relationship as described by Leila.

The dream takes place at an institution of higher learning. We can view this in two ways: 1) as a symbolic place where "higher learning," consciousness understanding, can take place, or 2) a rational, intellectual attitude toward what the institution of marriage "should" be. The dual aspects of the college campus symbol point to both what is possible and what is problematic in their relationship.

The opening scene shows the possibility of conscious growth when Leila wishes to leave the wheelchair; in other words, she contemplates standing on her own. However, viewed from the second association, the marriage is crippling to the individual stance of both Leila and her husband. Each partner depends on the other and both are obliged to move in the same direction by artificial means. Neither partner can stand on his or her own two feet. The relationship is symbiotic.

The situation characterized symbolically by the marriage partners being confined to the same wheelchair is more prevalent in our culture than we care to imagine. When we use worn out stereotypes of what a marriage should be, we are in effect crippled in finding our individual path. We fall into role playing and easily become stuck in a "husband" or "wife" persona, merely actors in the staging of a marriage.

Marriage *can* be an institution that facilitates conscious growth, provided it is built on mutual respect and love. The support found in such intimate relationships can enable each partner to realize their individuality, but inevitably this entails a disruption of old patterns. When change happens it is difficult to accept, for we are caught in our attachment to the person we envision our partner to be. When our expectations are not met we feel betrayed. Attempts to "save a marriage" are misplaced if they neglect the need to save the individuals involved. It is necessary to forge a relationship between two unique persons as opposed to one between roles based on expectations.

Leila wanted to leave her crippled state within the marriage, the fixed idea of being taken care of by "a good man." Although the bus is not a vehicle where one travels one's individual route, one can at least make a personal decision about where to go and how to get there. The bus stop Leila sees in the distance may be viewed as a potential way to travel down her psychic road. However, the threat of rain delays the desire to move.

Rain is a cleansing element coming from the sky; it is the necessary moisture that penetrates earth or matter to enable growth. Without this cleansing and moisturizing element, our body/matter is without spirit; it becomes hard and dry, as does one's outlook on life. Although the fear of standing on her own, finding her own direction and feminine strength are seemingly paralyzing factors, the dream ego sees another option: the bus stop is within sight. Waiting for the "bust" (a Freudian slip!—a symbol of feminine nurturing qualities, par excellence) suggests something of the nature of what is to come.

Leila

Prior to beginning analysis, my husband and I had numerous sessions with an Episcopal priest as counselor. We each blamed the other for our dissatisfactions. Gritting my teeth with determination to save the marriage, I had attempted to discipline myself to touch him whenever we were together, to listen, careful not to interrupt him, and to make my own decisions so that he would stop thinking of me as a nitwit. He had announced that he would no longer initiate sex because of the countless rejections he had experienced over the years.

For our twenty-fifth wedding anniversary we had decided to fortify our union by restating our vows with a couple who had married the same year. At the last minute, when preparations had been made and invitations written, I reneged. This was one of my initial efforts to honor my wishes over those of others, and I nervously explained that I could not affirm our marriage because it was built on promises I now questioned. Days of impressing anyone I could with the sanctity of my Christian wifehood had begun to wane.

Since that time I had of course been aware that our marriage was in trouble, but I had not grasped the deplorable state of affairs pictured in the dream of the wheelchair.

The autumn after the dream, we spent a weekend at an exclusive mountain resort. Waiting to be seated for dinner, I looked around the room filled mostly with older couples. The women were smiling placidly as they listened to the men. I heard several tell outrageous tales, and the men seemed to be charmed by the frivolous innuendoes.

While we ate, two women at the next table excused themselves to go to "the little girls' room," and I was struck with the accuracy of the euphemism that I, too, often used. Maidens still, they functioned to make the men feel important. I had been in similar dining situations on scores of occasions, and for the first time recognized that the cloying sweetness in their faces was a characterization of their lack of substance. My husband and I were the same—I was a princess-wife bound to him for my strength.

Contemplating this scene, I began to accept the sorry state of my marriage. To learn to walk on my own I would have to give up the search for myself as reflected in my husband's pleasure. In being so entirely identified with my princesshood I had made him my prince-consort, and though afraid of losing the man himself as I renounced my role, I had to release him. Gradually, I opted to risk it in order to find out who I really was. This was the first step, but I would soon dis-cover how deeply ingrained was my princess-wife portrayal.

As we continued our sex therapy, the tension was almost unbear-able. I threatened divorce more than once, trying somehow to pro-voke him into making me a passionate woman—as if this were his responsibility—and he was angry at me for not receiving him as a man. Both of us were indeed crippled.

*

The dreams presented so far occurred in the first three months of Leila's analysis. There were many more during the following months, continuing the same themes of redeeming the closet child, meeting the conflicts of the marital situation, and being visited by animals.

Leila's outer life was in a state of upheaval. She was questioning her relationships with family and friends, realizing that the old ways of relating were a false front. She experienced much loneliness as she was becoming more estranged both from the self she had once known and from others. This time was the beginning of the night-sea journey or desert crossing, as Jung describes the path of individuation. The old and worn-out ego structures were dissolving, and it was stressful to hold the tension of opposites between well-ensconced values and new ones arising from the unconscious.

By this time Leila was no longer taking tranquilizers and antide-pressants, so her senses and emotions were not veiled. It took many more months, eleven in fact, before she was visited again by the dark-haired feminine figure, as in the dream presented in the next chapter.

8
The Dark-Haired Girl

I am with my husband in an auditorium. He is disapproving of the way I'm sitting, my feet curled on the seat. We leave the meeting and I go to bed with a dark-haired girl. It is a very large bed. She is way on one side, and I am on the other. We are both naked. I tell her that since we are to be married soon, maybe we'd better see if we enjoy fondling each other's breasts. She agrees, and I love touching hers. I mostly fondle and suckle but a little. She has small breasts that look similar to mine. We both get very aroused. She wants to touch my pubic area, but I tell her we are both having our period and cannot. While we are fondling there is a tall, thin, stern looking spinster-type woman in an old-fashioned coat and hat watching us. I tell my bed-mate we cannot marry. She does not understand.

Leila often accompanied her husband to his professional meetings and this was her association to being in an auditorium. They would be there for his business, not for entertainment. In the dream she is apparently making herself comfortable, but her husband disapproves of her "unladylike" posture (which Leila dreaded in reality). Once she leaves her husband's cold, rational business world she can enter the world of Eros, the realm of feeling and relating. There she meets a dark-haired girl with whom she engages in mutually stimulating sexual activity. This girl (who later becomes the dark-haired woman again) is a shadow figure.

I reminded Leila of Jung's concept of the personal shadow—that it is comprised of all one's attitudes, values and instinctive desires that are incompatible with the ego-conscious image of who we think we are or should be, and therefore are repressed. Jung wrote:

> Everyone carries a shadow, and the less it is embodied in the individual's conscious life, the blacker and denser it is. If an inferiority is conscious, one always has a chance to correct it. Furthermore, it is constantly in con-

52

tact with other interests, so that it is continually subject to modifications. But if is repressed and isolated from consciousness, it never gets corrected, and is liable to burst forth suddenly in a moment of unawareness.[3]

The shadow has been termed "the dark side," and indeed can embody evil contents, or what may be felt as evil. But not all repressed material is malevolent; it is also unlived life. The shadow is an integral aspect of the personality and wants to live. Without conscious understanding of our shadow we are incomplete. What we fail to see in our own shadow—maladaptation, prejudices, ugliness, undeveloped talents—we project onto others. The more we fail to accept those split-off attributes of ourselves, the more one-sided we become, which is to say neurotic. Tremendous psychic energy—the same energy that could be expended in creative work—is required to suppress shadow material. Repression ultimately results in depression: we literally "depress" aspects of ourselves that are incongruous with our self-image.

The dark-haired dream girl, so opposite to Leila's natural coloring, is symbolic of her repressed sexuality. Developing from the image of the filth-ridden rat to the unbridled donkeys and the wild tiger, the symbol of repressed sexuality now emerges in human form, thus closer to consciousness. Although still adolescent, she embodies the natural yet confusing desires a young girl feels at puberty.

The dream brought to Leila's mind a time when she was twelve and invited a friend to spend the night. They were engaged in age-appropriate sexual explorations when Leila's mother entered the room. She admonished the girls and sent the friend to sleep in another room, leaving Leila distraught and very embarrassed. This traumatic experience created a deep psyche wound. All delight in her natural, sexual being was relegated to the shadowy unconscious; bodily pleasures became associated with something forbidden and dirty. This event marked the end of Leila's psychosexual maturing and accentuated her little-princess identification.

The dream had healing qualities. It takes us back to that traumatic

---

[3] "Psychology and Religion," *Psychology and Religion,* CW 11, par. 131.

time yet allows the dreamer to recapture pleasure in her body and in sexual feelings, instead of shame and remorse. We find now a close identification with the shadow component, both having small breasts and both menstruating, pointing to the possibility of new life. Ego consciousness is becoming more accepting of shadow attributes. This makes it possible for these repressed components to be integrated into conscious life. Leila and the dark-haired girl are to be wed—they are to become one, but not at this time.

As happened in life, the heavily veiled spinster attitudes of Mother burst through to have their say and to negate the possibility of feminine development. Injunctions from the personal mother, collected over the years, remained in a highly charged emotional complex still governing Leila's attitudes toward her sexuality. Edicts from this complex are no less controlling than her personal mother. We are left with the understanding that, until the tyranny of this complex can be overthrown, no uniting with the image of the dark-haired girl, and all that this image symbolizes, can take place.

Movement toward conscious realization generally provokes a countermovement from the unconscious. The autonomy of an unconscious complex is powerful and does not relinquish control without a fight. Modifications in consciousness, or we could say the advent of new life, followed by the counteractive force stealing these insights away, is a motif frequently found in fairy tales.

In the opening scenes of "Rapunzel," for instance, the king and queen are deeply saddened because they have no children. One day the queen yearns to taste an exotic plant she sees in the garden beyond the palace walls. The king steals it for her and later she becomes pregnant. The stolen, forbidden food belongs to a witch who lays a curse on the unborn child. At birth, the witch steals away with the baby girl and seals her in a tower.

We find parallels in Leila's psychological situation. The ruling principles are sterile; nothing fosters new life. The soul, psyche's kingdom, is dying. Beyond the conscious structure of fortified walls—that is, in the unconscious—wonderful plants of all kinds flourish. But food that is nourishing to the psyche and delightful to the senses has yet to be tasted. The feminine ruling principle recognizes this nourishment and the masculine ruling principle obtains it. There is a promise of new life, with embryonic formations of new attitudes toward self and others. Then, when these break through to consciousness, the time of "birth," the witch, representing the autonomous mother complex, steals it back.

Before the "wedding" or integration of Leila and the dark-haired girl—ego and shadow—can come about, the witchy mother complex must be confronted.

Leila

My elderly parents were failing rapidly, and I had no choice but to occasionally make the two-hour drive to help with their care. Panic still seized me, and at Nancy's suggestion, as my car turned that familiar corner, I imagined a circle surrounding my body to protect me from my mother's control.

The circle also served to prevent me from spilling forth accounts of my activities to her, a compulsion that plagued me through my teens and into married life. I had always faithfully reported the details of social events and organizational meetings that she had manipulated me to take part in. When she was due at my house, I would spend days rearranging knick-knacks on the tables and books on the shelves as she preferred to see them, cleaning everything in sight. Hearing her car in the driveway, I would frantically check myself in the mirror to make certain my hair was perfect. I lived for her compliments, and I never tested what would happen without them.

Safe within my magic circle, I relaxed enough to study her closely. Discoursing on the lives of others, she praised those who were always pleasant and fun to be with, those loyal to family and who showed good taste and kept a nice house. I writhed in my chair. Finally I realized that I had agonized to win her admiration, while constantly fearing that I would not, in her words, "measure up."

During subsequent visits, my shield firmly positioned, I continued to observe this person I now saw as a fat monster of platitudes. Obese most of her adulthood, she was afflicted with painful joints, and walking became increasingly difficult. I promised myself to stop paying attention to her. However, I soon realized that even when I wasn't with her, the harsh self-judgments persisted. Nancy pointed out that this fault-finding female existed within my own psyche, so I decided to kick her out.

With that, things actually got worse. I examined current photographs and flinched that my hair was not curled like my mother had always wanted. I cooked a meal but immediately became discouraged because it was not what she would have planned. I talked to a friend, only to regret my comments, worried that my mother would not approve. Such self-rejection emerged daily and, telling myself that I did not have to conform to my mother's standards, I struggled to ignore these intrusions. But try as I might, I could not. I had become her dutiful disciple.

When I recognized that the disapproving spinster-type in the dream was my mother, who had indeed stared down my budding sexuality, I was newly angry.

Consumed with loathing for this critical ogre, I wrote journal entries to confront her with the harm she had done by humiliating my young friend and me, the soul-crushing shame that had followed me through the years. I wanted to rip out her guts with a knife. Once I drew a bloated form and stabbed it with my pen, shredding the page. (Very much like the dream of killing my empty shell-woman.)

My hatred was not confined to my journal. I told anyone who would listen what a terrible person she was. Gradually, I understood that my misery was due to my negative mother complex, not the woman who had given birth to me. As hard as it was to separate one from the other, in time I grasped that my dependence on my flesh-and-blood mother was the witch stealing away any likelihood of my discovering vitality within myself. Much later I discerned that the influence of that immense knot of energy, the complex, far outweighed that of my personal mother and, in essence, ran my life.

Meanwhile I blamed the "queen" of my home of origin, as I had named her when writing about Princess No-Face. It was as if her watching eyes were everywhere, and I had no sense of humor about the situation. Furthermore, I could see her need to control me, but for quite a while I was not able to claim my own need to control others. I did not want to criticize, yet found that I often did, if not aloud then to myself. Exactly as my mother had done, I judged those close to me, feeling they would never "measure up." I caught myself shrewdly undercutting others by bringing the conversation around to what they were uncomfortable with in order to expose their inadequacies.

A loving heart does not disparage, but the negativity in mine took over, and I could only acknowledge this to myself. Over the years I learned that when I truly experienced the positive images in my dreams, the critical attitude lost its power.

One afternoon I had a startling insight. The nurse pulled the blanket aside to elevate my mother's feet, and her swollen legs were bared. The nurse told me they were as hard as stone and that rubbing them with medicated lotion did not soften them. Sickened, I looked away, and a myth I had recently read rushed to mind: the goddess Venus had turned women into stone because they disdained their bodies.

I asked the doctor about my mother's legs. He said he had never seen anything like them and did not know the cause. I did. In analysis, the disastrous results of denying my sexuality were becoming plain, and I was witnessing what might happen to my body if I continued like my mother. To the very end, until she sank into a coma, my mother denounced her legs, directing the nurse to keep them covered with a fluffy lap robe.

9
That Pot Is Boiling Over

I am washing my hair in an unfamiliar bathroom. A strange man with black hair and mustache comes in, sees me, then backs out apologetically. I follow him to say it is all right. I get into my bed and see the stranger outside my window. He is replacing broken window panes. He steps into my room and stands on my bed. I am angry and afraid that he will dirty the sheets. I walk out of the bedroom and pass a stove, commenting, "That pot is boiling over." Then I see a tremendous snake, flat-headed, rising out of the pot. I am frightened and run into a large wooden shed.

The dream opens in a bathroom, uncannily appropriate considering Leila's need to rid herself of "waste material" that continues to poison her body. Hair on the head is symbolic of attitudes, involuntary thoughts and fantasies. It is also associated with strength (as with Samson) and beauty (one's "crowning glory"). Washing hair is symbolically absolving oneself from the attitudes which contaminate or dull our strength and beauty. Leila's psychological hair-washing involved finding her inner abandoned child, exploring her sexuality and confronting her negative mother complex. When one is able to accomplish these difficult tasks, the cleansing process allows another psychic component to enter.

A stranger (although not as alien as the space men in her earlier dream) arrives unexpectedly. In a woman's psychology, the male stranger is an aspect of what Jung termed the animus, a Latin word meaning spirit. It is the contrasexual side of her psyche, her inner man. As with all archetypes, the animus has two sides. The positive aspect is that he enables discernment and concentration, and is often associated with a woman's creativity. He shines the light of consciousness on a woman's unconscious creative resources.

The negative side of the animus manifests in rule-bound assumptions and opinions and a need for power. The negative animus is also a destroyer of Eros, the principle of relatedness. When he invades and controls consciousness (and he does this subtly and seductively), the result is animus possession, which characteristically manifests as righteous indignation, argumentativeness, rigidity, debasing of others, nagging or mean-spiritedness—the very opposite of relatedness.

The man coming in through a "window" of consciousness is unknown to Leila. A stranger appearing unexpectedly is another archetypal motif often found in fairy tales. In "Beauty and the Beast," the stranger animus comes in the form of an ugly beast who promises an impoverished father great riches in return for his daughter. Because of his neediness the father relinquishes the girl. As promised, great wealth is realized. At the conclusion of the story, when the daughter can feel empathy and love for her beast, his curse is lifted and he is transformed back into a manly prince. The beast in the fairy tale is not unlike the space men in Leila's dream. He is that foreign, unconscious masculine energy which must be looked on with favor yet must be grounded in feminine consciousness lest it become possessive, as we find in another fairy tale, "Fitcher's Bird."

In this tale the stranger comes in the guise of a beggar asking for food. The impoverished father allows his daughter to give him a bit of bread, for that is all that can be spared. But as soon as she touches the stranger she is immediately transported into the basket on his back and carted away to his remote castle. Instead of riches to behold, there are bodies of dead women. In the end, the daughter, by using her craftiness, escapes the chamber of death.

The two faces of the animus are realized by a woman both positively and negatively in different situations. Like two sides of a coin, one aspect promotes psychological growth, while the other imprisons or possesses, leading to the death of a woman's Eros. Helpful solutions, new insights into old problems or an energetic burst of ideas, on the one hand, and destructive actions, cutting or snide remarks—even "innocent" innuendo—on the other, manifest the dual nature of the animus. Conscious attention to remarks or reactions that seem to break loose, spilling from her mouth in an autonomous way, helps a woman to differentiate the two aspects of the animus. In time, after many experiences, she arrives at a new understanding of herself and the masculine component within.

The salient point in both "Beauty and the Beast" and "Fitcher's Bird" is that the daughter or immature feminine (that is, the little princess) must leave the protection of father's domain lest she live psychologically destitute, never realizing womanhood. The father's domain includes not only the personal father's attachment to his daughter, but also patriarchal structures such as government, university, religious institutions and commerce. The actions of the animus always instigate change. He can bring the light of discernment, differentiating feminine Eros from masculine Logos, or he can cut a woman off from Eros, all those attributes that are expressions of one's soul as it relates to others.

Returning to the dream, the stranger animus comes as a window repairman; that is, he replaces those shattered or cloudy panes that obstruct our view of outer life. Returning to bed, the dreamer wants to close her eyes to new aspects of herself (as in the dream of the closet child). But once she is enabled to see more clearly, her innocence, her place of repose, is no longer so clean and pure. She cannot remain unconscious of the changes coming about. When she leaves, she finds a pot boiling over, symbolizing intense heat or passion.

A stove is where we prepare food to give us sustenance and pleasure. We take raw materials and transform them into something palatable, digestible and nourishing. It is the same with psychological understanding. We take raw input, ideas or fantasies, and let them cook. There is a waiting time—no microwave zap!—for these events to be transformed into the right amount of doneness for our psyche to digest and derive nourishment from them. In Leila's psychological container she is cooking a snake, a tremendous, hissing snake.

Leila and I talked about the powerful and potent symbol of the snake. From earliest times the Uroborus—imaged as a snake eating its tail—has symbolized the cycle of life: birth, death and rebirth. This relates not only to physical life but to psychological life as well. Life in the fullest sense is a round, constantly transforming. Worn-out or imposed cultural ideals, passé ways of viewing life, outmoded convictions regarding womanhood, give way to new beginnings, imaginative responses and inspiration.

A similar association with the snake is found in Tantric practices. It is believed that at the base of the spine a latent power called Kundalini lies coiled like a snake. Through meditation and other disciplines this form of yoga aims at awakening the Kundalini so that it may ascend through the six progressive chakras, increasing in psychic power until enlightenment is achieved. The first or basic chakra, called *muladhara,* is located in the area of the genitalia, and through sexual response the Kundalini arises from its dormant state.

The snake is also symbolic of phallic or creative power. Paradoxically, since the coming of Christianity, the snake has been debased as evil, being the tempter in the Garden of Eden. Its phallic shape connotes masculine sexuality and that too is feared as evil.

In Leila, the formation of new conscious structures is apparently related to this potent symbol of birth, death and rebirth. The snake also implies the recognition of the maleness and male sexuality of the stranger animus and the potential for creativity. In the pot, the feminine vessel enclosing this strong masculine image, things are cooking, change is happening. New images are coming to consciousness. Although Leila in the dream continues to run from the situation, we are assured that there is monumental movement in the psyche.

Leila

My desire to respond to my husband's lovemaking was ever present. Yet, despite my efforts, shame of my body and fear of his persisted. Often it was as if my body shut down and my ardor drained away, leaving me helpless to continue. On the eve of this dream I had attended a special prayer service and knelt at the altar railing to ask the priest for the laying on of hands for my wounded sexuality.

Fantasies of passion soon obsessed me. I felt something slither up my torso, but I did not connect it with the snake in the dream until

Nancy and I discussed the Kundalini. My dream ego had run, but nevertheless my imagination was engaged. The sexual snake was never far away as I envisioned it wrapping itself within and around me. Though at times it felt like there were three of us in bed, communion between my husband and me was enhanced during this sensual period. I came to appreciate that serpents are also regarded as good omens and blessed the one in my dream pot.

I read about the chakras, intending to memorize them and move myself along. But I soon conceded that my intellect was not going to do it for me and closed the book.

The stranger with the mustache reminded me of a villainous figure, yet he was kind. Who was he? I really had no idea.

Bungling along from day to day, I fought against conceiving of myself as a clumsy, stiff-limbed adolescent groping in the back seat of a car. As I moved toward accepting this as my psychological reality, my judgments softened. I sat at my kitchen table imagining my closet child, Ann, now a teenager, in the opposite chair. Crazy as it felt, I talked with her as if she were a beloved daughter and let her ask about her sexuality. We laughed gently at her ineptness, and I gave her understanding. I began to cherish this girl, so uncertain, so vulnerable at this phase of her development.

I thought back to when, working with the dream of the closet child, I had heard her sobbing, then hurried to buy her a baby doll. At that time I had seen myself, the woman, and myself, the weeping child, in the mirror. I had questioned which one lived. Now I understood that they both did, side by side. Likewise, both the woman and the adolescent girl sat at the table of my consciousness.

Meanwhile, being involved in my fantasies, I blamed my husband a little less for my problems. Whenever I came near to being as simply myself as I could be, blood pumped from my pelvis and I treasured it as holy. I was learning that the way to a man's heart is through a woman's passion for her own heart, and mine I pictured between my legs, beating up through my whole body—the promise of the snake in the pot—my Kundalini.

10
The Clay Mirror

My husband and I are driving down a dirt road. There are many side roads, but we cannot find the right one. There are city street signs out in the country, and I find this incongruous. My husband is impatient. I am puzzled. We ride and ride, on and on. He bangs his hands on the wheel. I am constantly looking for the road we need to take. There is a terrible rain storm.

Now my husband is no longer with me and I am in a parked car with several lost children I have found. I am drenched and huddle with the wet children in the car. Then I am in the driver's seat, again drenched, but I am now a man. I see a small round hand mirror outside in the rain. I pick it up, bring it into the car and see that it is not a mirror but a round flat circle of clay. I cannot see my reflection.

In this dream, the feeling-tone of being lost in some forsaken place paralleled the emotions Leila experienced in her outer life. She was confused and disoriented, feeling, "I know not who I am. I know not where I am going."

The dream reflects the husband's position—he is in the "driver's seat"—an arrangement Leila did not question. Even after much searching, the way appears unclear for both. Which road to take? What is their ultimate destination? They are in the country, an unknown, less developed place. The city street signs offer no help and only add to their confusion, for their familiar names suggest the cultural center from which they came, not where they need to go. They feel hopelessly lost, reflecting the situation in their married life.

Alone, she gathers the lost children, several children, as if the grief of the closet child has now multiplied. Here Leila is not afraid of the rain, as she was in the wheelchair dream. She is soaked through and through by the fertilizing sky spirit, as are the young growing aspects of herself. When she changes her position to the driver's seat, Leila

63

finds herself as a man—using her inner masculine attributes to take charge of her own direction, although still not moving forward. Then she discovers the clay mirror fashioned from earth, in which she cannot see her reflection.

Making a deliberate move into the driver's seat, being enriched by the fertilizing moisture of the masculine spirit, gathering in the lost creative essences of life and caring for them, these are forward-moving steps on Leila's path of individuation. They are giant steps in contrast to the marriage wheelchair dream. Paradoxically, although she is consciously making great strides, Leila feels stuck—as if her car is mired in the mud. The old image of herself has been erased, but a new self-image has not yet formed. She stands betwixt and between what once was and what is yet to be. It is that very difficult, yet very necessary, time in analysis when one feels lost and at a loss.

Leila

I awoke with an almost unbearable sensation of nothingness, as if life were pulling at my right hand, death at my left, and I could join neither. In despair, I realized that I was still the shell woman. Even with the progress I had made, I had not rid myself of her.

To reenter the dream, again and again I would sit Indian fashion on the bed and curve my fingers into a circle. Peering at it, I saw nothing. This clay mirror symbolized the void I was experiencing.

Though Nancy defined it as an image of hope, I was petrified to find myself in such a state and could not imagine anything positive coming of it. I strained to adopt her faith as I studied this dream, telling myself that since my hands were holding the clay, surely I could mold it. Doubt won out, and after years of thinking I would soon be healed from depression, I steadily sank into what seemed a bottomless pit. I hung on to my trust in Nancy and her trust in my psyche, but still feared for my life.

I mustered my energy to enroll in a ceramics course, believing that touching actual clay might help. We began by throwing it on a wheel. Unable to keep my hands steady, and not liking to dirty them, I did not return after the second class. I regarded this failure as evidence of my inability to construct my own likeness from the earth, and my despair doubled.

Meanwhile, to avoid perceiving myself as a nonentity when others announced their crowded schedules, I kept busy. I could then check my watch and say, "I have to go to visit for the hospital committee," or, "I'm due at the library to tutor." It seemed to me to be a pretense because in reality I just wanted to type my dreams and try to decipher them. Incapable of comprehending that this was in fact my present life, I saw myself as sick and inferior.

I was having a great deal of difficulty orienting myself. (I knew that I needed to come down to earth, but despite logic, I was not sure it was there and felt unconnected to it.) Nancy often suggested housework, and this infuriated me. Was I not fit for something worthwhile? Yet surprisingly, the rhythm of polishing silver, washing dishes by hand or cleaning the toilet—particularly the toilet—grounded me.

One day the question, "Are you my mother?" came from nowhere, insistently, like a familiar tune. I remembered a book by that title that I'd read to my kids. It was the tale of a baby bird falling from the nest and journeying to look for its mother. So here was Ann's story, plus that of the lost dream children, trying to find me, their mother.

Shortly after the dream, with no design in mind, I grabbed four brown socks and stuffed them with rags, tying them into the shape of a rabbit, I then hid it in a drawer under a pile of clothes. Hurrying to retrieve it the first morning I was alone in the house, I chastised myself, "Grow up, Leila." I could imagine Ann whispering, "Don't take my earth-bunny from me." Sensing the sacred in this request, I declared aloud, "Go to your bunny, my child. It won't be taken from you." I dug it out of the drawer. "Are you my mommy, earth-bunny?" I asked. Hugging it close, I was consoled.

Part of me considered my actions crazy and yet another part demanded to speak through them. Conflict between the two seemed unending. I had to risk the craziness.

To soothe the neglected children, when I was alone I would pore over the book and stroke the rabbit. For the following months this crude facsimile was my comfort in the midst of my emptiness. As if holding a shell to listen to the sea, I cuddled it between my shoulder and ear to hear the ground. This little animal toy was beloved. I had made it for my inner child, yet it was more. I used a piece of the earth, depicted by the brown socks, to create a symbol of the Easter season, exactly as I would eventually form my psychic clay into a new vision of myself.

On Easter morning I drove out to the beach, and in the drizzle that soon soaked me I walked and wept for a couple of hours. When I was calm, I started home. Several miles down the highway a hitchhiker—a tall, slender, dark-haired young woman in an orange raincoat—stood by the side of the road. Alert to the danger of giving a stranger a ride, I sped by. A short distance further, without thinking, I made a U-turn to open my door for her.

She climbed in beside me and said that she was trying to get to her church to sing in the choir. Nearly there, we sat in a line of traffic at a swing bridge that was stuck. With the probability of a lengthy wait, both of us damp and cold, we pulled into a McDonald's. Between us we had just enough money for coffee. Inside, staring out at the rain, I felt comfortable with her, though we spoke hesitantly, not even exchanging names.

Later I reviewed this chance meeting. What had prompted my abrupt turnaround? Perhaps because I identified with her, a lone woman making her way. Could I do the same, fully as solitary as she? Had I, in her, encountered some true essence of myself? I only knew that being with her had been more meaningful than the hallelujahs I had previously sung in services of worship.

Inevitably, after savoring my progress and feeling that I was taking more responsibility for myself, I experienced inertia. Nancy and I could only agree: "We'll have to wait and see what comes."

11
The Garden Wall

I am seated at a wooden table with a friend and ask her how her mother is. She says her mother is losing weight because she won't eat. I get on the floor with my friend's daughter. We put out our hands to each other —mine are small like hers. I measure carefully and am surprised. Then I am outside in a garden that has a big brick wall at the back. There is a small bush with bright red blossoms, like passion flowers, growing on top of the wall. I walk to the wall and place a stick by the bush. I see my friend's mother drive away in the car. Then I see a large tree growing in the corner of the garden. The wall ends by the tree and I can see outside the garden through the openings between the limbs of the tree.

Leila's association to the friend (a woman she knew) was that she was very much like herself, living under the stifling influence of her mother. Leila's hands remain small and childlike, rendering her unable to metaphorically grasp or embrace the new developments within herself. But it is a promising sign that the mother is losing weight—the emotion-laden autonomous voice which governed Leila's conscious life is losing strength. Although still confined by, or up against, brick walls, she finds a passion bush and with concerted effort reaches to the top of the wall. (Neither Leila nor I knew if there was such a plant as a passion bush.)

Only when the mother drives away (or when we can drive the mother complex away) does she view a great tree at the end of the garden. This is the cosmic Tree of Life, rooted in the underworld while its branches reach upward to the spiritual realm. The same could be said of our psyche. Our roots lie in the unconscious, nourishing healthy psychic growth and spiritual understanding. The great tree is also symbolic of the Tree of Knowledge, of consciousness.

Leila's situation parallels the story of Adam and Eve eating from the Tree of Knowledge. Once she started to become conscious, she was cast out of her Garden of Eden, that innocent, childish dependency and belief system.

A wise old analyst frequently said to me: "You must leave the Garden of Eden before you can arrive at the Heavenly Gates of Jerusalem." I said the same to Leila. Through its spreading branches she views the world outside her Garden of Eden, her previously limited vision of life now expanded. Once Leila was able to experience her emotional instincts (all symbolized by the passion bush)—love, hate, sensuality, fear and joy—she found a sense of interiority, a depth of meaning. She found her soul.

Leila

Waking, I lay in bed listening to my husband's razor clang against the wash basin. Burrowing into the pillow, I wanted to hide and sympathize with the wooden neurotic I knew myself to be. I floated in limbo, unable to remain this person, yet incapable of moving on.

Suddenly remembering that my dream ego had paid tribute to the red passion flowers, I jumped up, determination throbbing through my limbs. I knocked on the bathroom door to invite him to shower with me. Once the water touched her, Ann was apprehensive. As my arms encircled his waist and our skin met, I took a big breath to soothe her/me. Respect for myself for undertaking this demanding task began to replace my impatience.

I understood that I had been in the Garden years and years too long. I had to forego the presumption that, if I were good and sweet, things would go well for me. This naive approach to life wasn't valid, and I had to be careful not to unconsciously slip back into it. Yet in my concern for the lost child within, I was constantly confused about how to tend to her growth and at the same time experience my life as a middle-aged woman. Each day I sorted out my predicament as best I could, resolving to trust the messages of my dreams.

This particular dream told me that my escape from the Garden was through my own passion, and in my approaches to my husband I pictured myself placing the branch on the wall beside the red flowers. With a private ceremony I could relax and receive his caresses. His arms supporting me, I relished the safety in which I could learn the language of sensuality.

When shame from the past emerged, the scene with my childhood friend and terrible mother figure flashing into consciousness, I would lose my confidence. Reaching for the dark-haired dream girl, I imagined us playing in bed. My yearning made me bolder and more innovative. I planned lovemaking, both with her and with my husband, with enthusiasm.

I was beginning to come to terms with the fact that I had lived in the fantasy world of the little princess all my life. In giving up this masquerade I was stranded much of the time, unable to relate to my husband or to others. My previous value system was crumbling and I had no new creed by which to live.

12
Refugee

I am in the forgotten space under a large cathedral. I see several people imprisoned in a stone-like cave with an iron gate across the entrance. One is a strange little bald-headed dwarf-like man with thin legs. He is the curator of a museum. I enter the prison-cave to talk to him, then turn just in time to see the gates closing to imprison me. I barely escape before the gates close. I run from the cathedral and join a crowd of refugees on a wide road. I do not know where I am going, only that I must go. Some refugees get into cars. I become frantic because the cars are leaving me behind. There is no room for me. One car needs a baby to satisfy the quotient. A dark young woman dressed in a sari pulls a suitcase from beneath her robe, wraps it in swaddling clothes and says that it is a baby. The swaddled suitcase is passed into the car. I am encouraged by someone in the crowd to push my way in. I am surprised to see, as the clothes drop away from the suitcase, that it is really a beautiful baby.

Leila's sudden impulse to stop for the hitchhiker a few days prior to this dream was perhaps synchronistic, for the young woman was like a refugee, alone on the open road.

This dream reminded me of the old cathedrals of Europe with crypts in sub-basement areas, dug into earth and lined with inscribed sarcophagi, often showing the likeness of the renowned person inside. These crypts were dimly lit and musty. The ambience of the cave underneath an exalted external religious structure was not unlike Leila's situation. Psychologically she was entombed, lifeless and stony, while outwardly she personified a grand edifice of piety and grace.

The personal unconscious is like a museum, a storehouse of images and feelings. The dwarf-like man, keeper of these relics, reminds us of the fairy tale ogre who lives in a cave, or under the earth among the roots of trees.

Dwarfs are a frequent image in women's dreams, and symbolize a critical psychological function. In Greek mythology, certain dwarfs were called dactyls, meaning fingers, and therefore they are associated with creativity. We often find these characters in fairy tales, where they have a positive function as craftsmen, or miners of precious gems as in "Snow White and the Seven Dwarfs." They are those helpful masculine agents which bring invaluable assets, creative resources buried away in the unconscious, into the light of consciousness. In other stories the dwarf is a malevolent figure, irritable and demanding, who steals the treasure, as in "Snow White and Rose Red":

> There once was a poor but kindly woman who lived with her beautiful twin daughters at the edge of a forest. So lovely and sweet were these young girls that she named them for the rose bushes which grew outside her door, Snow White and Rose Red. One evening a knock was heard at the door and upon answering it they found a huge bear. He was polite and asked if he might come in out of the foul weather. The old mother felt sorry for him. She invited him in to stay by the fire and offered him food. The girls enjoyed his company and played with him as with a giant toy, rolling over his massive body and snuggling into his shaggy coat. When spring came the bear announced that he must leave to guard his hidden fortune from the mean-spirited dwarfs who lived in the roots of the forest trees. They had been asleep for the winter but now were awakening with the spring thaw.
>
> One day when the girls were gathering sticks of firewood, they spied a little creature hopping up and down. As they came closer they found a dwarf with his beard caught in a log he had been splitting. The dwarf sputtered and hurled insults at them for standing there gaping like ninnies. Rose Red took scissors from her pocket and cut a portion of his beard to free him. Instead of being grateful, the dwarf was incensed that she had ruined his beautiful beard and shouted degrading names at them.
>
> Shortly after they came upon the dwarf again. His beard was entangled in his fishing line and he was in danger of being pulled into the sea by a great fish caught on the end of the line. Again Rose Red took her scissors and snipped off more of his beard. "You goose-heads!" he screamed, and ridiculed them soundly. On another occasion, they saw a giant eagle who had the little dwarf clutched in its talons about to fly away. The girls

wrestled him free, and once again they were repaid for their help with only outrage and scorn.

The dwarf was successful in stealing a bag of gems from a bear, but the twins came upon him chuckling over and admiring his cache. So enraged was the dwarf that he puffed up, turned red in the face, and started jumping up and down. He was unaware of the bear who had arrived on the scene. The bear quickly did away with the dwarf and then was redeemed from a curse. The bearskin fell off and a prince in golden array appeared. In time Snow White married the prince, Rose Red wed his brother, and with their mother they all lived happily together in a new kingdom.[4]

The dwarf here is a paradigm for how the negative animus functions. Regardless of what the woman accomplishes, however great her success, his scolding, critical voice is constantly there: "You're not good enough, smart enough, pretty enough; you'll never make the grade." He is insatiable in his demands and relentless in his negativity.

The malevolent dwarf in Leila's dream is not unlike the dwarf in the fairy tale. He captures the woman by denigrating her abilities. He oversees the deadly domain of religious dictates in the dim recesses of unconscious life, those early injunctions barring Leila's psychological development. Imposed attitudes such as sweetness, compliance, gentility, piety and feminine virtues related only to motherhood, are the death knells of a woman's instinctive nature.

This is not to say that such attributes are not beneficial when authentic, but when enacted as a role they are superficial and sentimental. To identify *only* with them stands in the way of realizing deeper strength and meaning. There are equally as many times when assertiveness, spontaneity, playfulness, sensuality and creativity are called for.

In the tale of Snow White and Rose Red, the dwarf steals the treasures of the bewitched prince who appears in the form of a bear. Likewise, the negative animus steals the possibilities, value and power of the positive animus. When this happens in a woman's psychological

---

[4] Grimm Brothers, *The Complete Grimm's Fairy Tales,* pp. 664ff. (paraphrased).

life, she becomes just as irritable and demanding as the dwarf. She has no humor, no fluidity, and views things only in black and white. Like the dwarf, she has an unconscious standpoint of demanding the right and the need to be served. No doubt this was a strong aspect of Leila's mother's animus, too. She was imprisoned, possessed, by the angry, greedy and demanding dwarf animus.

Women who are unconscious of the negative animus often repeat the ways of their mother and become just as destructive to their daughters and others, all the while hating what their mothers did to them. How often we see our mother in ourselves, hate it, resist it, but cannot control it. We open our mouth and out pops the mean-spirited dwarf!

The negative animus is a sign that creative gifts are not being used (as in the tale, riches are stolen and buried beneath the earth) and libido is dammed up. We leap up and down in argumentative entanglements, unconscious plots, manipulation or a sense of martyrdom. The remedy comes when we set the animus to work in some creative endeavor. Then we will not contaminate our daughters, but rather mirror for them a more constructive side of the feminine. Thus, we could see that the question for Leila was how to put her animus to work. The answer, though, was still not clear.

In the dream, Leila narrowly escapes imprisonment by this negative unconscious influence, and rushes to a place where refugees are gathering. To be a refugee means to leave one's heretofore safe haven and strike out on the uncharted path, without the accustomed comforts or social status. This is analogous to the path of individuation.

Leila now must leave behind the superficial prop of her social life, for it has become uninhabitable, even dangerous. A new place of psychic refuge cannot be found without discomfort, discontent and frustration. Leila's words in the dream—"I know not where I am going, only that I must go"—show her dedication to this arduous task. She is frightened of being left behind and a "quotient" must be met to allow her passage. Perhaps here Leila meant "quota" but quotient was the word she wrote, pointing to a factor that has been divided, or a fraction resulting in the division, the psychological split, that must be recognized before she can be on her way.

The dark-haired woman appears at the right time in the right place once Leila is committed to her journey. She is wearing foreign dress because she remains "foreign" to conscious understanding, yet she contains the essential "quotient," the split-off factor, that will allow Leila to leave. Leila must now carry her own baggage, weighty and burdensome though it be. As she accepts this responsibility, the burden is transformed into a new-born baby in swaddling clothes. This image recalls the Christ child at birth, and therefore can be considered a symbol of the Self, of unity and wholeness. The new-born baby is the embodiment of new life that will accompany her on this journey. The commitment to be responsible for this child is where the work begins.

Leila
Opening my eyes, I frantically repeated the dream words: "I do not know where I am going, only that I must go." The idea of joining up with refugees had a great impact on me. I recalled pictures of men, women and children leaving their homes, taking only what they could carry. Running from oppression, searching for shelter, they hid by day and moved by night. Their faces were sad, yet strong with the determination to keep going. I had always wondered how they could possibly survive. Now I, too, had no road map and no choice.

Much of my conflict was the result of the inner battle between opposing natures—the refugee and the princess. I worried that the princess had the power to order the refugee executed, yet I sensed the inherent strength of my cloaked traveler. She was the one on whom I could depend to protect me from the demands of the negative mother complex. She was an exciting figure for me and brought me courage over the years. Thus began my calling as a refugee.

My family and friends didn't understand the urgency I felt for change. Their platitudes echoed in my head:

"Many aren't so lucky. You should count your blessings."

"Smile and you'll feel better."

"You should get out of the house. Volunteer and be useful."

"Stop feeling sorry for yourself. Do something for someone else."

These were the oppressions from which my pilgrim-self needed to escape. Despite resolutions to stop pleasing others, amounting to many New Years' worth, I failed. What is more, when I tried to buoy myself up, the very platitudes I was trying to ignore welled up inside me and I became false, unable to speak from my heart.

Nancy's observation that all along I had been doing the right thing for the wrong reason would bring me up short. I began to give myself permission to do whatever I desired at the moment, as inconsequential as playing solitaire or sitting on a park bench in the sunshine. I felt strong when alone and not following the crowd.

Though a refugee is often forced to travel alone for days on end, I worried about spending much of my time apart, and of course also worried about what others would think. Nancy reminded me of the fairy tale woman who stayed alone at her wheel to spin thread from raw material. I took comfort in understanding that this was my chance to weave my own fabric of life.

During one session I said, with apprehension, that I had not known on that Easter Sunday, when I turned to pick up the dark-haired hitchhiker, that I was agreeing to become a refugee. Nancy replied, "Yes, but She did. If we believe in divine intervention, that is."

Realizing that my encounter with the young woman in the orange raincoat had presaged my existence as a veritable outcast gave me the stamina to tolerate the difficulties. Over the years I would discover that therein lay both my strength and my excruciating isolation.

My declaration, "I don't know where I'm going, only that I must," came constantly to mind. I watched people of different ages, seemingly sure of their destination, stride by my window. I envied them, but it was futile to pretend that I knew mine. No longer at home in my surroundings, I grew to appreciate the accuracy of the metaphor of the refugee. I consoled myself that as slow as my journey was, no one could make good time in such circumstances. Sooner or later I would comprehend the message from my dreams. They still kept me con-

nected to the reality of my inner life, and recording their images was central to my days.

While struggling with loneliness, I was encouraged to think that our marriage was no longer stuck in a wheelchair, and that I was standing somewhat on my own. Yet try as I might to squelch her, the princess-wife continued to wreak havoc. Animosity often reigned. I was convinced that if my husband would just opt out of the marriage, I would be all right. I was irritated watching from across the room as he sat contentedly reading the newspaper. Neat in a suit and tie, his briefcase by his chair, he seemed filled with purpose. I saw him as "the enemy."

Often when he would mutter the simplest how-are-you, I would experience condemnation and quickly withdraw. I was confused by my ambivalence toward him. Some mornings when he was going to work, afraid of losing his support, I would beg him to delay. On others, I would be glad to have him gone. Viewing him as smug in his pragmatic masculine world, I resented my suffering.

To shut this wife up, I decided to stop communicating with him unless absolutely necessary, and the ensuing silences were miserable. I was caught between the princess's inane chatter and the emergence of the dwarf animus from under the cathedral, cutting my husband down with cleverly disguised sarcasm. I cringed as I realized that I was every bit as controlling as my mother. Fortunately, I was learning to express most of my negative thoughts only to myself, journaling page after page, not spewing them out.

I was beginning to distinguish a natural feeling that would come, as if wandering up from my gut, reminding me of the Kundalini. Though still foreign to me, I tried to welcome each authentic emotion as a valid guide to my truth.

*

As Leila's account of her emotional life indicates, her journey was very difficult; there were many washed out bridges and dead-end roads. She was a wanderer in no-man's-land, often ending at the place from which she started. Once she disclaimed the princess attitude, the negative dwarf animus was constantly present; his irritability, authoritarian demands and self-righteous indignation all surfaced with a vengeance.

The word "animosity" derives from the word animus and this seemed to be her pervasive feeling. This can be the breaking point of many a marriage or other close relationship, because the negative factor is projected onto the significant other in our life and we define him or her as "the enemy." In this case Leila's husband represented what she was incapable of establishing for herself: a sense of self-confidence and independence. She was, however, developing the ability to stand outside herself, as if observing herself on a screen, becoming more objective and self-aware. She gradually began to withdraw her projections, claim her own limitations, and reduce her habit of fault finding.

13
The Gigolo God

I am in a swanky nightclub, sitting with the tall, lanky owner/entertainer. He leaves me at the table and goes to dance with a pretty dark-haired woman. They leave the club and I follow. He takes her out for air then leads her to a low wall. They straddle the wall, facing each other. I am horrified to see that he pulls her to his chest, stroking her hair and quoting a Psalm to her. I realize that I have always been invisible to the woman, and now I am invisible to the man.

The swanky nightclub setting suggests a place dimly lit, glittering with sparkles and bubbly champagne, alcoholic "spirits." It is an ambience designed to dull our rational attitudes and intoxicate us with another reality. It is a place and time for seduction.

I am reminded of Herman Hesse's book, *Steppenwolf.* The protagonist, Henry Haller, a professor steeped in the world of the logical mind, epitomizes the world weary soul. He does not know how to live nor does he know how to die. Late one evening, ever so dismal and forlorn, he enters a nightclub and finds a magical place. As if Fate takes over, he meets a woman who brings back memories of his youth and love. She teaches him to dance and to make love. He is caught in a whirlwind of change.

In Leila's dream, although the gender is reversed, we find a similar situation. Desperate to live her life more fully, yet unable to let the old attitudes die, she was existing in limbo, like the earlier test tube dream woman.

Reason and sobriety, associated with the god Apollo, are overwhelmed in the nightclub scene by the world of Dionysus, god of wine and ecstasy. Dionysus's domain is related to the irrational (beyond the rational), the sphere of emotions, instincts, sensuality and imagination. In our modern, rationally ordered world, the Dionysian is often considered base and inferior. Chaos and pandemonium describe the realm of this god, for he is ever changing. He represents a force of nature that challenges staid ways, that would bring to life what is dead in us—and yet is restrained by our fear of change, our eternal timidity, our need for approval.

Creative energy often upsets existing psychic structures based on collective attitudes and values, but it also encourages new beginnings and exhilaration. The dream image of the nightclub owner, who Leila spontaneously called a gigolo "god," corresponds to the traditional attributes of Dionysus.

The "gigolo god," or Dionysian animus, leaves the dream-ego to dance with the dark-haired woman. It is the dance of life; moving to life's rhythms, feminine and masculine motions complementing each other, swaying in unison. It is as though movement comes about only with the dark, repressed side of Leila's sexual nature. I think of a folk hymn, "Lord of the Dance," which tells of the creation of the universe. Dancing with the god is a creation of oneself.

When the dance is complete, the dark-haired woman is taken out for "air." Air is also symbolic of spirit, the *pneuma;* it is the life-giving force as we "inspire" it. The animus as a psychological entity is spirit, which brings inspiration. He can bring creative ideals with clarity and purpose once we are receptive to his movements and rhythm.

The man and woman straddle the wall, thus leaving their sexual parts unguarded. While caressing the dark-haired woman's head—that is, Leila's thoughts and images of feminine sexuality—the man recites a Psalm. Leila was unable to recall the particular Psalm or its meaning, but generally speaking the Psalms relate to solace and divine guidance. It shocked Leila that something deeply moving and spiritual could enter into such a profane, erotic atmosphere! The dream ego views this with a sense of horror, as if a great sacrilege has occurred. There is no conscious comprehension that what is sacred can be correlated with, and complementary to, what is sexual.

This dream came about eighteen months after the beginning of analysis. As we can see, the unconscious is introducing a new concept, namely that spirituality can coexist in harmony with matter or body. That is the dance. Leila's previous one-sided attitude of what is spiritual—certainly not the body—is being challenged. Unlike the previous animus images of alien men spreading juices and the window washer, this nightclub owner/entertainer has a spiritual dimension.

Dreams have a compensatory function in the self-regulation of the psyche, in that they bring to the surface images of all that is repressed, neglected or unknown, leading one toward a perspective quite different from the conscious attitude. This dream of the gigolo god introduces a new archetypal concept in the form of Dionysus, who embodies spirit in matter. Jung writes, "The divine powers imprisoned in bodies is nothing other than *Dionysus in matter.*"[5] Instinctual responses or awareness are Dionysus dispersed in body.

In ancient times women were initiated into the mysteries of Dionysus. An exquisite and well-preserved frieze in vibrant colors decorates the walls of the initiation room at the Villa of Mysteries in Pompeii.[6] The scenes portray the woman initiate as she progresses through the stages of the ritual. First she is told the stories of Dionysus, his dismemberment and rebirth. She then presents her sacrifice at the altar where older priestesses receive it. Now, all alone, she proceeds into the world of instinct and nature—young boys and animals. Silenus, a demigod, plays a lyre. He is said to have been the protector and mentor of Dionysus.

Then follows a scene that depicts the initiate hurriedly turning around to face the way she has come, as if startled by something unseen or not wishing to go deeper into the mystery. Her face is filled with fear and one foot steps out of the picture frame. She wants to flee. She is divested of her outer garments, left with only a shear sheath covering her body. The initiate is about to enter the realm of Dionysus who along with Ariadne presides over the ritual. They are

---

[5] *Aion,* CW 9ii, par. 243, note 19.

[6] See Qualls-Corbett, *The Sacred Prostitute: Eternal Aspect of the Feminine,* pp. 70ff.

centrally depicted on the back wall. And it is frightening. The initiate must reach within to experience her life dismembered and then to re-member it in a new way. The old pattern of life is no longer valid.

The story told in these scenes cannot be grasped by intellect alone, but must be felt in the body—the instinctual fear and pain, yet also the ecstasy, of an encounter with the numinous. After entering a de-spairing, lonely place, the woman could then gaze upon the veiled phallic symbol, fertilizing instrument of the god. It was not without risk, however, for the initiate could become so enamored of this new-found power that she might compromise her feminine nature. It is then that the dark-winged goddess descends with a whip in her hand. There is no place in the new, re-membered psyche for hubris or ego inflation. The initiate feels the sting of the whip on her bare back as she buries her head in the lap of an older woman, one who has previously been initiated. In the final scene we see the woman, serene, in new clothes. An older woman is combing her hair. Eros is standing by with a mirror that reflects the woman's changed image.

Today we do not have such rituals to guide us through our psychological process. Nevertheless, our psyche still provides a similar experience through our dreams. In this dream, Leila glimpses a new understanding of the interrelatedness of spirit and body. She also sees that this inward journey is an arduous one. There are times when she wishes to flee, not unlike the Pompeiian initiate, yet she stays, committed to her statement: "I know not where I'm going, only that I must go."

Leila

I had long been vaguely aware of a sensation of invisibility. I certainly had the impression that my mother was looking right through me, more interested in what my husband said or did than in what I thought or felt. Yet I also considered myself to be unnoticed and left out with friends or acquaintances. I usually tried to convince myself that this was absurd, but it had persisted.

The gigolo god in the dream brought me a picture of my dilemma.

The horror and hurt cut into my chest, stealing my breath, as I stared at him embracing the dark-haired woman. They each had something I lacked.

The solution to my problem came unexpectedly.

For years I had yearned for a male friend, a man with whom I could talk, sharing my quest. A man I could really trust. I imagined us at lunch, our heads almost touching as we earnestly spoke to one another. For this to happen I needed to change the way I related to men. Not understanding how to do this, I simply wished and wished.

Then Paul came. Hearing of his illness, I walked to his house several blocks away. He was an acquaintance who had been the subject of much gossip, and as we settled down in his richly furnished study on that first morning I fought my moral judgments. In his fifties, he was battling cancer. During subsequent visits, in the study or beside the pool, he talked about his youth and broken relationships, the loss of his professional practice and his fear of death. He was a handsome man and I was strongly attracted to him. His emotional pain made him real, and I liked myself when I was with him. No longer the child cowering in the corner, I spoke up, sharing my own deeper feelings and perplexities. I was seen. Often my depression lifted in his presence, and once home I sometimes danced alone in the den.

Though we never lunched, we drank many cups of coffee while I treasured his companionship. But he weakened and I realized that our times together were numbered.

I watched his widow and children from the back of the crowd at the graveside. Compared to their relationship with him, how could I have supposed that our meetings had been meaningful? After all, we had been close for only a brief interval. True to my negation of myself, I concluded that I had been my old goody-goody self, that my desire for a male confidant had tricked me into thinking that my connection with Paul had somehow been different.

14
Card for Paul

I find a greeting card on the ground. "For Paul" is written on the cover. Inside there are drawings of the moon in its various phases.

Leila's new-found way of relating to a man is illustrated by the card she finds. The moon, long associated with goddesses of love, brings a soft glow of consciousness, a diffuse light very different from the stark glare of solar consciousness which corresponds to the masculine way of perceiving and dissecting. Although Leila was unaware of the moon goddess aspect of the archetypal feminine, that energy nevertheless moved within her. When a woman is comfortable with her womanhood, then moon consciousness shines through her. Genuine caring for another is possible and evident.

The feminine principle of Eros, or relatedness, is that which bridges and unites. It manifests in mediating, facilitating, reaching out or receiving—not in polite words, the correct expression, expected roles, Leila's relatedness was heartfelt. The message to Paul and to herself was the moon in all its phases.

The moon reflects not only a woman's physiological reproductive phases, but also her psychological fertility. There are times of waxing and waning, of shining forth or disappearing. In the dark moon phase, it is important to contain one's "witchy" moods so as not to be destructive to self and others. Becoming conscious of our moon phases allows integration of the archetypal feminine.

As with the gods of ancient myth, archetypes are polymorphous. Their many facets speak to the range of our emotions and behavior. Considering the depth of feeling Leila experienced with Paul, it was natural for her to feel the stinging loss of his death. Aphrodite, goddess of love, embodies both grief and mourning. At the death of her beloved Adonis, it is said that the mountains echoed with her cries.

Leila

My connection with Paul had been as brief as the dream itself. To assure myself of the significance of our visits, for awhile I carried in my pocket the story of the dream, like a talisman.

Slowly I absorbed the card's message—that the phases of the moon reflected the development of my feminine nature, enabling me to relate with love. In reliving my moments with Paul, I realized that I had indeed responded sincerely to his honesty. My warmth had flowed to him. I had not been coy, covering emotional distance with silliness. Again and again I thrilled to the dream and to my remembrance of Paul. He was, for me, truly a Dionysian man. And so began my dance with the god. I was no longer invisible.

Over the ensuing months I discerned that in essence my association with Paul had shattered my rigid idea of the manner in which a man and a woman should behave toward each other. Through the years the importance of this basic understanding has worked its spirit into my consciousness.

After my experience of the gigolo god, both inwardly and with Paul, a spark of well-being would often surprise me, easing my way a bit. I welcomed the relief and braced myself for further changes.

One day I looked down at the skirt of my pink dress printed with tiny navy bows. Suddenly seeing it as princess attire, I jerked it off and threw it away. Pink represented for me the prudery that had weakened my passion and paled my personality. I promised myself never to wear it again. I shopped tirelessly for clothes to lay out on the bed before I posed in them before the mirror. Having found the styles I would no longer choose, I was unsure which I would, but I was always drawn to bright colors.

15
Femme Fatale

In this dream I have long straight black hair and a sleek look. My skin is smooth and glossy and I have long painted nails and dark eyes. I am a beautiful brunette in a foreign place where war is being fought. I am with the troops and confused most of the time because I can't tell which soldier is the enemy. I wear black stiletto heels and a tight red skirt. It is hard to run to avoid the enemy fire. Then I am in a hotel with a dark man. The man is handsome and I am attracted to him. He asks, "Wine or bed?" I answer, "Both!" Then I check the mirror and note that even though my red skirt is pulled to stretching across my wide hips, I am very beautiful. I am aware of what covers my breasts—a black silk bare-shouldered affair with tiny straps —very sophisticated. I pick up a jacket and crook my finger at my friend and entice him toward the front door. He follows me and as we open the door, the police are there to arrest him. I had tricked him.

Trying on new clothes, seeking an outer appearance that complements a change within, Leila's self-image is fluctuating and uncertain. The dream ego has integrated aspects of the spirit of Dionysus associated with the dark-haired woman: sensuous tight skirt, bare shoulders, wine and sexuality. She is in a foreign place, for such a self-image is still very strange to her. She appears to be something of a camp follower.

In her waking life Leila felt the raging war as the conflict between old conscious attitudes and new images storming in from the unconscious. This conflict is termed the "tension of opposites." Consciousness must not win the battle, yet it must not lose. Leila is neither a prim housewife nor a camp follower. Tension must be maintained between these opposites in order that a third element, the transcendent function, may develop.

The transcendent function is a manifestation of new energy, often in symbolic form, that does not identify with one side or the other but incorporates elements common to both. It mediates between the opposites, providing a bridge between consciousness and the unconsciousness. It offers the possibility of synthesis.

However, there is an ominous and menacing factor surfacing in the dark-haired woman's character. She is a seductress who tricks the man, a siren who uses feminine wiles for power or gain. Like a prostitute, she betrays the essence of Eros, using sex in a malevolent way. This is not unlike what we find in Homer's *Odyssey*, where the seductive Circe gains power over men by turning them into swine; that is, sexuality is used for purposes other than expressing love or pleasure.

Symbolically, the siren is the dark side of the moon, an archetypal, shadowy aspect of feminine sexuality that is present in every woman. The woman not conscious of this side of herself may win many conflicts using her sexual charm, yet betray both her lover and herself. In the end she risks losing the very essence of herself, Eros. When a woman becomes conscious of her feminine nature, there is a release accompanied by a sense of power which can be used in either loving or destructive ways.

This dream presents another psychological challenge: the dangerous interplay between the femme fatale shadow and the stranger animus, a fighter. When they become too closely aligned, these unconscious factors can provoke mischief, even destruction. The creative libido is seduced into a power play which eventually imprisons all developmental progress.

The dream came a little more than two years into the analysis. Leila's outer appearance was changing almost monthly. The gaunt frame of the anorexic was replaced with a soft, rounded body. Her clothes were brightly colored, often casual jeans with a loose sweater and comfortable shoes. Although not black-haired, her hair style was such that the natural wave gently outlined her face. A new beauty shone in her face, replacing the previous haunted look. At times her eyes reflected a delight in life, and she could laugh. I am reminded of the attributes of Aphrodite: "radiant goddess, lover of laughter." Yet the dream shows that underneath the radiance there lurked a dark, vengeful, power-hungry aspect of the feminine.

Leila

After work my husband routinely drove to our weekend house eighteen miles away, often for the night, while I stayed at home. Though aching to be his lover, with my ambivalence toward him I didn't know how to begin. I thought my troubles would be over if only I had the nerve to divorce him and be rid of my role as wife, but finally I faced the hard reality that I would not do this because of the complications involving our family. So what could I do about my misery?

One day, glancing down at my neglected hands, I admired my older daughter's elegant red nails and made an appointment that same afternoon for her beautician to apply acrylic overlays. I selected the color Rose Musk. With strong polished nails, my confidence grew.

Two weeks later I stood at the door to welcome my husband home from a trip. We embraced, and as my fingers smoothed his hair I imagined myself to be "the woman with the rosy claws," who led him upstairs for slow, intense lovemaking.

Valuing the freedom gained by having acknowledged Princess No-Face and my closet child, for a year I kept my dates with the manicurist. Recording my glimpses of this rosy-clawed woman, I came to feel that she was close to the dark-haired girl.

One afternoon my husband and I finished pruning banana plants and laughed as we hugged, our arms sticking together because of the gummy juice. The woman-with-the-rosy-claws said, "I'm glad for the new life between us," and led him to bed.

That Christmas he climbed down the ladder to plug in the tree lights. "That's done. Ready to decorate?" he asked.

"I'd rather make love," I replied, and we carried wine upstairs. I sensed an exquisite presence with us. Was it the dark-haired woman? I lit the candles, hoping for the support of my claws as I caressed my man. Later he napped, and thankful to have discovered that I could, in a sense, divorce myself as wife and reunite as lover, I lay quietly

beside him. With him, I would use my tongue more for kissing than talking. From then on I thought of him as "my man" instead of "my husband." I was able to see him, not as a stereotype but as an individual. This made a big difference in my treatment of him.

The femme fatale in me had been trying to make herself known for quite a while, and when she broke through my resistances she was indeed powerful. Striving for the sleek, sophisticated look I had in the dream, I was exhilarated and felt I somehow glowed. Ideas for trysts with my husband came easily. I really enjoyed making suggestive comments to him and his friends.

My femme fatale occasionally embarrassed me. In working on plans for a new house, the architect requested ideas for the master bedroom. The rosy-clawed woman blurted out, "A Jacuzzi and a bed for lovemaking. Nothing else." Feeling the fool, the princess-wife blushed. Embarrassment, I soon saw, was preferable to the fact that invariably, like a mirage in the desert, my rosy-clawed woman would vanish, and along with her, my passion, leaving me empty and depressed.

Claws definitely have a negative connotation, and I was later to realize that I was too intrigued with what they represented in me. Nonetheless, at the time, with delight seeming to emanate from their movements, they encouraged me to move away from my princess-wife fixation. I really liked myself when I was using them. Having focused for almost three decades on commitment to marriage, my passion was exciting. (Over the next few years the dark-haired woman taught me to make love in order to connect with another, but not to seduce.)

I worried that my rosy claws would not continue to thrive, for as I've said, they frequently deserted me. Or so it seemed. Actually, as essential as they were for my poise, as princess-wife I still rejected them. The conflict raged on.

The yearning to develop the feminine in myself was constantly present. I wanted to welcome the goddess who personified this principle, as I was beginning to understand it. Yet when the urge came to do so I swallowed it, refusing to utter a name without a face.

16
The Virgin Mary

I tend a baby who lies on a table before me (bathing it). The baby begins choking. I am desperate because I know that I cannot save it. A beautiful woman in flowing robes comes up behind me and takes the baby into her arms. It stops choking. She sits down and holds the baby in her lap. I see her flowing robes. She is the Virgin Mary. I am filled with more gratitude than I have ever known before and turn to her and say, "I will serve You and Your Child."

Leila was tending the baby with caring concern; it was the new dimension of her psychic life. To neglect "the baby" would be to revert back to superficial ways of relating to self and others, or to negate the feelings and emotions sensed within her body. With the same soulful concern that she was first aware of with Paul and his illness, she could now engage with the malignancy she found in herself. The negative voice of the critical dwarf, the voice of "shoulds" and "oughts," diminished.

As with caring for an infant, inner work is often tedious, for it requires constant attention in order to allow the new life to manifest as it was meant to be. The unique design of each person is contained within the archetype of the Self, whose purpose is served by the ego. The archetype of the Self represents one's fullest potential and the unity of the personality. Jung writes:

> The self is not only the centre, but also the whole circumference which embraces both conscious and unconscious; it is the centre of this totality, just as the ego is the centre of consciousness.[7]

---

[7] *Psychology and Alchemy,* CW 12, par. 44. [In the *Collected Works* the word "self" is not capitalized when referring to the central archetype in the psyche, but in later Jungian writing it is conventional to do so to distinguish it from the ego-self.—Ed.]

The Self contains the encoded seeds of Creation's design, which seeks to be realized through the individuation process. While delighting in her new image as "the woman with rosy claws," perhaps Leila became too identified her. Overidentifying with an image is the opposite of integration. It does not allow the tension of opposites, but simply becomes one-sided in another way. Leila's former self-image as a prim and pious woman is replaced by that of the femme fatale.

The path of individuation is serpentine, not linear—it twists and turns. As we have seen before, it is a balancing act—many aspects of psychic life need to be recognized at the same time. Diversion from the path of wholeness often results in startling dream images. This dream alarms us, making us ask, "Why is the baby choking?"

Choking may be caused by something too large to swallow or a reflux of food that is partially digested. We say that "something went down the wrong way," meaning the air passage became obstructed. As with food, psychic matter can have the same effect when we take too big a bite. Too big a bite of the woman with rosy claws did not go down the right way. Thus, the baby is not getting enough air—*pneuma* or spirit. Sexuality is not mere instinctuality, as depicted by the woman with the rosy claws, but contains a spiritual component as well. Jung notes:

> It is an open secret that although physical and spiritual passion are deadly enemies, they are nevertheless brothers-in-arms, for which reason it often needs the merest touch to convert the one into the other. Both are real, and together they form a pair of opposites.[8]

While finding delight and joy in her long-repressed sexuality, Leila had not yet realized its spiritual dimension. Understandably, Leila dismissed the patriarchal structures which were responsible for her initial feelings of disdain toward body, sexuality and the spiritual aspects of feminine nature, yet this created a void. The image or energy of the gigolo god, that which embodied both spirituality and sexuality,

---

[8] "On the Nature of the Psyche," *The Structure and Dynamics of the Psyche,* CW 8, par. 414.

was not integrated in conscious thought.

Through her reading, Leila was aware of the growing movement among some women to find the divine feminine within themselves. Consciously attempting to replace patriarchal religious belief structures with those of a matriarchal source was futile for Leila. But she did seek a focus for her spirituality. Where might she find it?

Leila was not of the Catholic faith, and other than at the Christmas crèche the Virgin Mary was not emphasized in her Protestant teachings. Nevertheless, Leila's image of the archetypal divine feminine was that of Mary. This is not surprising when one remembers that during the early years of Christianity attributes once ascribed to the goddesses were assimilated into the characteristics of Mary the Mother, especially those concerning childbirth and children. The virgin goddess Artemis, although we mainly associate her with the hunt, was also the goddess present at childbirth. Likewise, another virgin goddess, Athena, commonly known as goddess of war and the development of urbanization, was also responsible for child care.

During the Middle Ages, when the Cult of Mary was prevalent, infertile women, or those with a difficult pregnancy or ill children sought her blessing. Mary served the same purpose as the ancient Earth Mother who assured the fertility of crops and herds and indeed life in all its forms. Today, in several European cathedrals, the statue of the Madonna is black, dark as earth itself, as if the divine feminine has not lost touch with body and matter.[9]

Another important amplification is relevant when considering the image of the Virgin Mary, especially as it relates to healing the split between body and soul. In 1950, Pope Pius XII announced in a proclamation of dogma that both the body and the soul of Mary were assumed into heaven. Jung considered this a psychological advance in that the masculine Trinity now incorporated a feminine component.[10] Also there was an acknowledgment of matter/body. The Virgin

---

[9] See Qualls-Corbett, *The Sacred Prostitute:* pp. 153ff.
[10] "Answer to Job," *Psychology and Religion,* CW 11, pars. 743f., 748f.

Mary represents both body and soul, soma and psyche, serving as a mediatrix between these polarities. She is the divine feminine aspect of the Self wherein these opposites are contained.

When an aspect of the Self shines forth in a dream one feels a sense of awe. For Leila, the dream had this numinous quality, both frightening and comforting at the same time. It stayed in her mind over the ensuing weeks. What did it mean to serve Mary and Her Son? She was reminded of the pure and pious countenance of Mary from Sunday School pictures, an image she emulated for many years. Did it mean that in order to serve Mary she would have to deny her newly discovered sensuality? Her fear was that she would have to become as "virginal" as Mary. Of course this was confusing.

In our discussion of the dream, Leila and I spoke of virginity in metaphorical terms, the meaning of psychological virginity, rather than chastity, as the word "virgin" is commonly used. Psychological virginity means being responsible for one's own beliefs, decisions and interactions with others. It is living in accordance with the inner authority, an awareness of the Self. This presented Leila with a dilemma: "How does one serve the divine feminine nature of the Self?"

Leila
Waking with my heart racing, I lay motionless to relive the dream. I was deeply moved that the Virgin Mary had come to rescue my psychic baby. My gratitude, as ardent as it had been when actually encountering her beauty in the dream, burst often into my thoughts during the following weeks. Her blessing loomed larger than me, larger than my life.

Nevertheless, I was dismayed at the vow my dream-ego had made: to serve Her and Her Child. To serve, in my training, was defined by what a Christian woman should be, and I did not want to backslide into my compulsive ministering to others to win their approval. It was impossible to get the Sunday School version of Mary out of my head. What in the world had I promised? Nancy and I decided that maybe I could ask the Virgin herself, but I left that analytic session not at all sure that I would be able to do so.

As I had when working with the Kundalini, I continued to look out-side myself for answers and decided that I would go to the authorities, meaning books. I made a few notes from the Bible and from Marina Warner's Alone of All Her Sex, but soon lost interest.

I was disappointed that a full-bodied Aphrodite had not appeared. The goddess of erotic love seemed to be more in keeping with my rosy claws, which still fascinated me. I associated the Virgin Mary with my girlhood innocence, as when, wearing a white robe, with a blue cloth covering my demurely bowed head, I had played her for the Christ-mas pageant. How could such a holy one support the unfolding of my sexuality and help me value my earthiness?

Finally I faced the fact that it was Mary, not Aphrodite, who had come. I began to think of her as "she who came in my distress." My reverence grew. In spite of my confusion, I noticed changes in myself. At times my kindness—with no falseness that I could detect—surprised me. The nagger in me did not as readily tell my husband what he "should" do. I found less to berate him for and was able to lighten up on myself a bit, saying inwardly, "There goes that princess-wife with her shenanigans . . ."

I left my manicurist, in effect removing my rosy claws, and instead visualized the dark-haired woman in order to gain the confidence to communicate with my man eye-to-eye. Her zest for relatedness filled me, easing the strain, and I began to speak from a rooted quietness. I felt more womanly and there was a gentleness about me, a genuine softness, yet with a subtle strength.

I still questioned my vow. After several weeks of pondering the dream, I dared to ask. Drifting off to sleep, I whispered, "Virgin Mary, how can I serve you?" When I awoke, I heard: "To serve me you must celebrate your life." Wondering if I had heard correctly, I echoed, "To serve me you must celebrate your life." Yes. I hurried downstairs to have breakfast with my husband.

More often than not, when I intended to repot plants, weed the garden, or bake bread, my enthusiasm would drain away. At such *times I would recall Mary's charge: "Celebrate! Celebrate your life!" In a flash, I would be flooded with well-being and know that there was nothing finer than to hold the dirt or dough in my hands. Without a doubt, this virgin pointed me to myself. I constantly sought to understand who she was for me, and at last designated her as goddess, hoping she might become that. In time, she did—"The Virgin Goddess named Mary."*

I had the urge to go to church, to kneel and praise the Virgin— exactly, as before, I had glorified Jesus. This behavior was fixed in me, and it took a great deal of effort not to revert to it. Again and again I recalled the words telling me to celebrate my life. Had I misheard? Uncertainty hounded me, but I reminded myself that Mary had not demanded that I worship her life. She had invited me to honor my own.

My thankfulness lingered and enriched my daily activities. At last I could appreciate the fact that the analytic process was holding my feet to the fire, readying me for transformation. Through the coming years, the Virgin's words continued to resound in me, returning me to myself as her gift gradually embedded itself in my soul.

17
Stitched from Beneath

I do not know where I am, but sense that I am deep under the earth. It is dark. I have found a treasure in a cardboard box. A funny little fat man who reminds me of a bald and shaven Santa Claus holds the box in his lap. I kneel in front of him and open the box. It contains large folded squares of a burnt orange cloth, on which are printed small squares, ready to be cross-stitched. I look up at the little man who puffs out his cheeks and bugs his eyes in wonder. He nods yes to me. I pick up a square of the cloth, turn it over, and find the most delicate, most precise and most beautiful single gold and green cross-stitch. Next I find crosses stitched on cloth after cloth, increasing in size, with more background green and solid gold crosses. My little man and I marvel. As I rub the cloth I find the secret of the crosses. The stitches have been stitched on top of the cloth and underneath at the same time. This is a discovery of great importance. No one else knows this cloth is so special, so beautiful because of the stitching from beneath. Only I know this.

Then I realize where I am—in a tomb. I hold a small china music box and look down at the little orchestra of china figures on its top. They are making music. Then the figures become human and life-sized. I stand in a darkened doorway watching them play. I must discover who did it. I notice a dark-haired woman, a member of the orchestra, but standing a little apart. She holds a triangle high in the air. As she strikes it, the triangle says, "Karen did it. Karen did it. Karen did it." The woman turns and faces me. She is exquisite. She frightens me, and I run from the tomb.

As in the dream of the refugee, the setting is underground, a place of darkness symbolic of the unconscious. However, the circumstances within this dream present an entirely different story. In the previous dream, the dreamer must escape the gnome-like image that tries to imprison her. That gnome or dwarf embodied the negative voice that overwhelms one with self-denigrating messages and destroys one's sense of self. This underground is no longer a place of entrapment, but a location of hidden treasure. The image of the gnome-like figure is also transformed. The little man ("a right jolly old elf," she said) is associated with Santa Claus, bringer of gifts. He allows the dreamer to observe her buried treasure, gifts of the Self, archetype of wholeness.

It is not unusual to find the most precious belongings in common wrappings or in obscure places. Think of the pearl hidden within the hard-shell oyster. In humans too, our real treasure is hidden by a crusty exterior, caked with the muddiness of personal complexes. It is difficult to reach, and one must dig deeply.

The outline of crosses needing to be completed on squares of burnt orange, and the gold crosses on green squares, reflect the symbolic meaning of the treasure. Burnt orange, a mixture of red, yellow and brown, indicates the blending of the red of passion or feeling, the yellow of thinking or intuition (instinctive knowledge) and brown, associated with earth or fecal matter—shadow contents we consider offensive. The interweaving of thinking and feeling, and the acknowledgment of body/matter (shadow) lends a specific coloring to the personality. This is the fabric of Leila's life.

In the dream the pattern is imprinted on the burnt orange cloth, but as yet the gold threads have not embossed it. Burnt orange also connotes the color of autumn, a beautiful time of year. We speak of "the autumn of one's life," which is applicable to the dreamer's age. In the second half of life there remains work to be done, new designs to be completed—encoded markings to be embellished. Green is the color of spring's new vegetation, fresh and lush.

One could say that the dreamer's psychological development is budding forth, awakening from a barren winter. It has not as yet achieved maturity, a time when the fruits of life are harvested. The delicate, precise, gold and green cross-stitching indicates each thread of our life. We create our mark, as it were, with each interaction, each relationship, be it with inner or outer aspects of life. It is our personal gold, which resists tarnish and decay.

The image of the unique pattern, with stitching from both above and below, reflects the interconnectedness of inner and outer experience. An ancient alchemical dictum illustrates this:

> Heaven above
> Heaven below
> Stars above
> Stars below
> All that is above
> Also is below
> Grasp this
> And rejoice.[11]

The starry constellations our ancestors saw as projected images of heroes, gods or animals, representing aspects of the divine, are likewise inherent in the archetypal images of one's psyche.

The dreamer now realizes she is in a tomb. Again, as in the dream of the refugee, she is in a place of death. Unlike the previous dream, she is not about to be captured but is visiting the tomb, the last remains of an aspect of herself that was buried. We bury—that is, repress—psychic contents that are in conflict with conscious attitudes or values. The challenge is to find these repressed contents and return them to the light of consciousness.

In the tomb Leila discovers a small china music box that then becomes a live orchestra playing music. What first appears as fragile, cold and lifeless, now is fully human. The music is the harmony and rhythm of the soul. It is preverbal, instinctual and universal. Music reflects feelings. The dark-haired woman is responsible for the sounding of inner emotions. She rings a small triangle that sends the message, "Karen did it."

The triangular shape is associated with the *yoni,* a Hindu symbol for feminine genitalia. To produce the clear resonating sound, the triangle is struck by a small rod; thus, symbolically, it is the combination of masculine and feminine images that produces music.

---

[11] "The Psychology of the Transference," *The Practice of Psychotherapy,* CW 16, par. 384.

Recall for a moment an earlier dream, "The Dark-Haired Girl," which related to an experience Leila had at the age of twelve, when a friend spent the night. Leila's mother sent them to separate beds when she discovered them engaging in sexual exploration. The friend's name was Karen. The tingling sound of the triangle played by the dark-haired woman is a gentle reminder of what Karen did—not in an accusatory way, but to bring that experience back to consciousness. The fragile china doll has transformed into the dark-haired woman and this figure, in turn, becomes an exquisite woman, but still the dreamer cannot accept this as a reflection of herself. This new image, which the unconscious is attempting to make known, to redeem, continues to be incongruent with Leila's conscious picture of herself, thus she flees in fright.

Leila

Stunned by the beauty of the dream cloth, the texture of the crosses lingering on my fingertips, I mused at length over the priceless gifts offered in dreams.

During a contemplative week on my own, I realized that since the dream of the garden wall, thanks to the passion bush, I had a sense of finally leaving the security of dependence. No longer would I be cared for by others, perhaps safe, but also confined. I sat many hours in awe of my secret with the little dream man. In exploring the meaning of "stitched from beneath," I realized that it filled me with the feeling that I was unique. The possibility of a personhood that had more to do with my individual soul and less with my various roles was real to me as never before. Weary of the empty charade of socializing, decorating and cleaning, all to please others, I could now begin to celebrate my own soul, as the Virgin goddess named Mary had instructed. Perhaps the purpose of my life was just that—my heartbeat, my very breath. As exciting as this was, I was still anxious, questioning who I really was and what I could be sure of.

In analysis, when I first glimpsed my entrenched dishonesty, both toward myself and others, I had struggled to renounce it. With unfore-

seen richness, my dreams were leading me to an alliance with myself, allowing me to be increasingly candid. How then to portray myself? I decided to trust my psyche to do so, which was a major step, though a decisive defeat for my ego.

Whenever I fell into the clutches of my old pattern of self-abuse, such as feeling badly about my comments to someone or worrying about my weight and wide hips, the attitude expressed by the cloth in the dream freed me. With growing awareness of its worth, I held my discovery close to my heart. With time, I became confident of being connected to the "beneath of things."

Yet by running away at the end of the dream I completely missed the important message that the dark-haired woman tried to convey. She wanted me to understand who I was, but I was not ready. Looking back, I perceived that my physical desire for my husband, which was becoming as sacred to me as the Eucharist had once been, was where I felt her presence. Not until years later did I connect it with the incident with my young friend Karen or with the dark-haired girl. I only knew that when I resisted expressing love toward my husband, I grew hardened. Then my mother's legs came to mind.

My dreams were gifts from the unconscious, yes, and I began to take responsibility for making them vital. I was also beginning to appreciate the difficulty of this. If I were willing to be immersed in my relationship to my dream figures, the marvel of another in my outer life, whether husband, child or friend, came leaping up from within, usually as a surprise to me.

Through the coming months I often relived this dream of discovering my secret stitches, experiencing again its grace and promise. My gratitude for the crosses themselves comforted me, and I was hopeful. My treasure in mind, I felt I was ready to be Leila, with nothing to recommend me but myself.

18
Dancing on the Milky Way

I carry a heavy brown grocery bag. I see a square one-room building with glass across the front, resembling a small store. A woman in leotards, a dancer, is inside the building demonstrating steps to a group. I think that I would like to try that. When I enter, she says to me, "I am going to play 'Tangiers' (or 'Tangerine') on the record player. You dance." I hesitate, becoming self-conscious, and reply, "But I don't know the steps." "Just move with the music," she counters. The music begins.

I listen a moment and say, "I can shag to that!" And I begin shagging. But I feel stilted. I decide to let my hips just move with the music. When I do I take off across the room, twirling and twirling. For a brief breath I am lifted into outer space, into the Milky Way. Then I am back in the building. I am me, but I am also in the others there. A disheveled woman comes in off the street. She wears polyester and jokes about it. She and I laugh about "green polyester." Two dark-haired girls stand in a doorway and make love. I argue with another woman behind a desk.

In dreams, in the most ordinary places, and with ordinary articles, extraordinary things can happen.

Leila hears music and although it is not a symphony orchestra, as in the previous dream, it is her soul's music—the title, "Tangiers," suggests something exotic. She listens to the rhythms and melody of her inner life. The dance is not the "shag" of her teen years, nor can she recapture its movements which are now false, therefore stilted. She cannot "think" dancing, that is, *know* the steps; she must feel the music and movement instinctually. She twirls like a dervish in a state of religious ecstasy, and is transported to the heights of the universe.

"He who knows the power of the dance, dwells in God," said Jelaluddin Rumi, founder of the dervishes.[12] The god in this case is

---

[12] Arianna Stassinopoulos and Roloff Beny, *The Gods of Greece*, p. 104.

100

Dionysus, who was said to have sung and danced in his mother's womb. The Maenads, his women followers, danced with rapture because they felt the power of the god within.

Of course, the Maenads' behavior was considered madness—leaving hearth and home, racing to the hills, dancing in the moonlight, suckling wild animals, and so on. Madness it may be according to conventional views, but such "madness" is not insanity but rather inspired movement to honor the god. The psyche knows no boundaries and such expansiveness can be experienced in brief moments of rapture. There are times when we feel an exalted sense of spirit, and become fully aware of the duality of our natural being, of spirit and body. However, one cannot live permanently on such an exhilarating plane; one must return to earth-bound matters. In the folk hymn, "Lord of the Dance," the lyrics are: "I danced on the moon and the stars and the sun, and I come down from heaven and dance on the earth." It is a song of creation, which cannot be lived out only in idealism or fantasy, but must be grounded in matter/body.

In the dream, Leila does descend back to earth, to the room from which she danced away. She is aware of herself and able to see different aspects of her personhood. She encounters an image of the ordinary woman, disheveled and "off the street," without grace or polish. Leila identified with this woman, so comfortable in the common fabric of her being, without feeling inferior. She could laugh about it.

The polyester specified in the dream is a synthetic fabric, not natural. It is analogous to the persona we "wear." We often enclose ourselves in a "man-made" attitude, which is different from and often in conflict with the natural fiber of our being. As previously explained, we do this in order to fit in, to receive approval and to protect our vulnerability. Our persona acts as our shield, and is appropriate in certain social or professional situations. But it is crucial to be able to differentiate the attributes inherent in the natural personality and those learned for social reasons.

In Leila's case, decorum and opinions sanctioned by her cultural milieu were her polyester suit—man-made and mass-produced. For years it served her well in gaining approval and to some extent allowed for ego stability. The difficulty came (as it often does) when she outgrew it, because she couldn't tell the difference between the suit and her own skin.

A Ukrainian fairy tale, "The Frog Who Was a Czar's Daughter," illustrates this kind of dilemma:

> There once lived a czar and his wife who had three handsome sons. When it was time for the sons to marry, the czar instructed each son to shoot a silver arrow. Where it landed they would find their wife. The two elder sons met with much success but the third son's arrow ended up in the possession of a frog. "Give me my arrow," demanded Ivan. And the frog replied, "Only if you marry me." The czar commanded that he do so. The frog and the third son were married but, of course, Ivan was very unhappy as the other brothers were blissfully mated. The frog, as she hopped after Ivan, told him not to cry, that all would be well.
>
> One day the czar commanded a contest to see which daughter-in-law was the most expert weaver. That night, when all were asleep, the frog threw off her skin and whistled for her three maids. They wove extraordinary designs, and when the czar saw them he was astonished at how beautiful they were. Then followed contests of cake-making and dancing, and each night the frog threw off its skin and accomplished the tasks in an astounding way. One night, becoming suspicious, Ivan found the frog skin and threw it into the fire. His wife was distraught because now, she said, she could no longer remain with him; she had been cursed by her father, another czar, and must return to her home kingdom.[13]

The story goes on to relate how Ivan, suffering much hardship, goes to the Thirtieth Kingdom and redeems his true bride.

This tale illustrates how women can be governed, in effect cursed, by the ruling dominant (collective "shoulds" and "oughts"). Not unlike man-made fibers, the princess's frog suit conceals her innate beauty and creative abilities. The frog suit, as our persona, cannot be simply done away with at the bidding of another, even a loved one.

---

[13] In *Russian Folktales*, pp. 16ff. (condensed).

Like a shield it protects until one is consciously in command of oneself. Leila, like the young girl in the tale, must learn to differentiate between when she needs to wear the frog suit, and when it can be removed. One could say that it is like the green polyester suit which grounds Leila in common, ordinary concerns.

The double image of the dark-haired girls reflects the aborted sexual experimentation between Leila and her friend Karen when they were young. Now, she is able to view and at the same time participate in embracing the young feminine nature, that lovely aspect of her instinctual nature which is certainly more than skin-deep. It continues to be removed—that is, "I am me, yet I am like other people," as if to say, "I can tell the difference between myself and others."

Standing in the doorway, a liminal space representing the threshold of consciousness, she has moved from the psychological space where she was, but has not yet moved into the space where she is going. She is betwixt and between, drawn to natural expression of body, sexuality and womanhood, on the one hand, and also to maintaining her ego identification with collective approval on the other.

The woman behind the desk is apparently an authoritarian attitude that wishes to control, like a teacher or a boss. With the acceptance of new images Leila is coming to accept her own authority, and when she hears the voice of past external demands she is, of course, resistant. But she does not run away. The ego is strong and remains in the situation to argue and defend herself.

Leila

I floated up from this dream to wander absent-mindedly around the house while reliving a childhood incident long dismissed and brought to mind by my night's journey to the Milky Way. When quite young, from my bed I gazed out the window at the starry sky and in an instant felt myself travel far above into a torrent of stars that joined into a blur of white. Overcome by wonder, I zoomed back under the covers. At fifty-two, I did not know what to make of my powerful imagination, but I was beginning to be more comfortable with it.

In the previous dream I had overlooked the dark-haired woman's message, "Karen did it!" Once again I ignored a vital part of the meaning of this dream—the frumpy woman in polyester. With my inner dishevelment, she was an apt personification. Seeing her as unattractive, I tried hard not to appear to be like her. Later I realized that this plain female, very much a part of my own psychology, was not shy about admitting difficulties with the practical aspects of existence, then dealing with them. I sorely needed her. I was definitely flying too high, and she was my ticket back to earth. It took me months to befriend her.

Yet I began to appreciate other women as I gained a sense of myself as a woman, or rather, as a composite of several—the disheveled one, as I called her, being one of them. Prefacing my statements with, "As a woman, I . . ." usually sent a shiver of delight up my spine and was enormously liberating, since I had avoided for half a lifetime the first person pronoun in order to induce my companion of the moment to talk about her/himself.

Soon after this dream my husband and I spent a weekend at the lake resort where several years previously I had recognized myself in the dining room packed with princess-wives. Walking alone one afternoon, I relished the rhythm of my body, and the phrase, "she walks in shameless beauty," occurred to me. I told Nancy what had popped into my mind, and she pointed out that I was referring to "she," not "I." I was able to allude to the "woman in my dreams," but was embarrassed to identify myself as her. I reconsidered my oath to serve Mary and her child by celebrating my life, and I now understood that the dark-haired woman represented my own femininity, manifesting in gladness on various levels.

Could I now truly receive my natural birthright as a woman? Through the following months I made progress as I discovered where my unlived feminine life lay hidden.

In the dream I had decided to let my hips move with the music, and I became more aware of them, without consciously connecting the dream image to my daily life. When making my bed and putting flowers on the table I realized that I had been swinging my hips. I had always believed that my hips were offensively wide, and I hadn't wanted to draw attention to them. Now, I found their swaying glorious. Moving them to country songs on the radio, I mopped the floor. While dusting, I created a wild dance. In the grocery store my hips swayed and my dangling silver earrings joined in. I really enjoyed matching my woman's rhythm to such chores. An inner voice roared that this was a waste of useful time, and I could only do my best to disregard it.

My hips seemed filled with life of their own, bringing me energy. I marveled that the portion of my body my mother and I had most disliked was the part that gave me confidence. It was as if my neglected life was materializing in my hips, and my poise waned when out of tune with their beat.

In certain situations, as when I was with three men in the lawyer's office for the closing of the sale of our house, the old feeling of invisibility threatened. Instead of posing questions in my best princess manner, I silently contacted my hips. Swaggering a bit to cross the room, I recovered my dignity. In touch with the strength in my hip-bones, I did not have to prove anything to anyone. If I opened my mouth to say hello and the princess-wife's cordial "oohs" and "aahs" escaped, I nudged my hips, and their swing sent her scurrying. Whenever my body became taut and I acted aloof, I wanted to weep with disappointment. Instead I moved my hips while intoning beneath my breath: "Swing, sweet hips." Almost magically, my haughty attitude slid away.

The joy stored in my hips was indeed my feminine nature, which I was gradually learning to trust.

Since this time I have dared to look under the princess-wife's skirt, so to speak, to confront my debasement of self. To myself I admitted buying financial security with sex, doled out with animosity. My prostitution of myself, meticulously clothed in respectability, had been as profane as the streetwalker's, and more dishonest.

19
Shaman

I hear a ghost playing an organ. Carrying a large key, I step through a ceiling-to-floor window that has no glass. I drop the key and look at it lying by my feet. Several women are choosing from a certain group of houses which one is to be theirs. A count is taken. There are more women than houses. I am told that I do not receive a house because I have to be a shaman. (I waken with a piercing pain through my head.)

Little of shamanism was known to Leila, other than that Native American rites were often performed by shamans. Their function among indigenous people everywhere, past and present, and the respect accorded them, were not known to her. The dream caused consternation and a pounding in her head for it was pointing in a direction of frightening isolation.

The eerie introduction of an other-worldly figure playing ethereal music places the dream in a realm outside known reality. She has a large key, the opener or decoding device to this strange place. I think the key denotes the meaning of the dream—the key to the unconscious; however, she drops the key and simply looks at it. The question remains, does she reclaim it?

In the previous dream she was standing in a doorway, on the threshold of consciousness, and now we find the dreamer stepping through the frame. She is moving out from the liminal space, stepping into an irrational reality. Our irrational life is not inferior but *beyond* the rational. I am reminded once again of the staid and rational Professor Haller in *Steppenwolf* who steps into the "Magic Theatre—Entrance not for Everybody." Leila, like Haller, leaves her rational sensibilities behind in order to realize the other-worldliness of the unconscious. It is not for everybody, for one must be able to endure a period of disorientation, which may feel like craziness.

Now Leila is separated from other women. She can no longer find the same companionship she had known before with her women friends.

I explained to Leila the role of a shaman in primitive tribes. At times an individual is designated at birth to be a shaman, or a sign or dream may come which designates their particular responsibility to their kinsmen. In either case, the shaman lives outside the tribal unit, set apart by his or her calling. Initiation rites into shamanism are frightening; they entail visions or dreams of dismemberment, followed by re-memberment. A symbolic death and rebirth occurs as the shaman reaches other-worldly planes. It is believed that the shaman can travel to the underworld to retrieve lost souls, or to accompany the souls of the dead to the upper regions. The shaman's spirit travels to all the realms of our psychic universe.

In certain native cultures today the shaman continues to be revered. For the most part our mainstream culture does not recognize the unique gifts (or the necessity) of the shaman. Nevertheless, they still live among us. They are the ones who undergo the intense descent into the underworld of the unconscious, who feel their ego structure torn asunder, who live close to their own soul's need rather than the expectations of the collective.

The dream of the grotesque woman in the glass beaker (told in the introduction) was a dream of dismemberment that occurred several weeks prior to this dream of the shaman. The earlier dream indicated that Leila's ego personality and persona were being dissolved in order that her psychic life could be transformed or re-membered according to her unique patterns encoded in the Self. Dreams speak to us in metaphorical language. The dream does not mean that Leila is literally a shaman. It does mean that, like the shaman, she has descended into the depths of interiority and has touched the well-spring of her being. In a manner similar to the shaman's initiation rite, she has experienced a coming apart of ego-imperative structures while allowing new visions to form. Living in two worlds simultaneously, she maintains the tension between them.

Leila

This dream intensified my confusion. Nancy described shamans as healers born into the position, meaning that they had been chosen. She advised me to let myself be set apart, adding that shamans some-times had a defining experience early in life. My childhood fantasy, so long ignored, of having flown to the Milky Way was perhaps just such a happening. Were the stars calling me once again? Did I dare refuse their message?

The previous dream about the Milky Way had reconnected me to that fantasy, and the shaman dream followed. Or had I misconstrued the dream voice? I argued with myself, my tremendous fear of being crazy almost defeating me. Looking back, I understood that my fam-ily's attitude toward psychology and imagination had fed the fear. This worry often surfaced.

Quite some time passed before I could allow myself to be in that other world, grounded enough to be sure that I was safe and sane. As the weeks passed I was preoccupied with my dreams and distant to family and friends. My loneliness was acute. Others seemed comfort-able with their lives, as if they knew what they were doing and where they were going, but I felt left out, cut off from everything. Allowing my imagination to roam sustained me. Christmas was approaching, and to relate my personal crosses from the dream "Stitched from Be-neath" to the season, I used the term "Xmas" rather than "Christmas."

Visiting the Metropolitan Museum of Art, I wandered through the crowd, uncertain which exhibit to enter, when suddenly a quote from a saint, her name forgotten, popped into my mind: "The true con-templation of any image is prayer." Surrounded by a profusion of images, I decided to pause at the entrance to a room until pulled to-ward a specific object. This cord repeatedly drew me toward render-ings of the Annunciation or Virgin and Child or The Mourning Virgin. All were painted by men. For many solitary hours over the next months, I pondered how I, as a woman, would portray her, for I saw doing so as celebrating my life.

My inner drama was surely a mystery, and if I did not constantly keep a dream vigil, waiting and watching, I lost the sense of myself. Accepting my need for dreams, I began to see the necessity of planting one foot in the inner world, the other in the outer. This delicate balance seemed beyond my capacities, and indeed several more years passed before I achieved it.

Was I hiding from myself? Many months later I realized that this shaman dream was telling me that I still identified with other women, wanting a house like theirs, a life like theirs. It challenged me to find my own individual way.

*

Considering Leila's earlier dream of Mary, and the feelings that drew her toward depictions of the Virgin, I think the following comment by Jung is worth noting:

> Analysis should release an experience that grips us or falls upon us as from above, an experience that has substance and body such as those things which occurred to the ancients. If I were going to symbolize it I would choose the Annunciation.[14]

---

[14] *Seminar 1925*, p. 111.

20
The Bird Launching

I am one of three women in charge of launching a bird into the air. We work in a round building in a conservatory, with rows of stacked seats holding a large audience. They watch as we try to figure out where to place the two final feathers that will enable the bird to fly. The bird, a big white beautiful thing, sits stonily on a hanging perch. We are perplexed and frustrated because there is nowhere to put these two feathers.

Out of the corner of my eye, I see above a window an empty perch hanging from a thick wire that has been bent into a circle. It has an attachment hanging from it that looks like a tiny bird-perch. Instantly I know that is what we need. I ask a man to reach up and unhook the attachment. He climbs a ladder and hands it down to me. We fasten the feathers. It works! The other two women hold the bird at the launching-tower window. I stand back in the doorway and I tell them to pull back on the swinging perch. They do, and it is thrilling to see the bird swoop away. I watch, trying to keep my eye on it, but since there are so many birds I lose sight of ours.

The three women who are launching the beautiful bird could be associated with the three stages of the feminine psyche: maiden, mature woman and crone. They also relate to Leila's personal story: her ego-personality, her shadow (that is, the dark-haired woman) and her analyst. The analyst is not necessarily me, the actual person to whom Leila tells her dreams; the image of analyst might now be internalized—her inner analyst. This image would relate to that psychic ability to look at unconscious images metaphorically and maintain some objectivity about them.

The dream's setting is a conservatory, a place where nature's beauty is on display or where beautiful sounds usher forth, like a music college. On the other hand, the word has the same root as "conservatism," where tradition and social institutions are valued more highly than individuation. Both are relevant here, as if moving from a stance of conserving old traditional values (the flightless bird) to the appreciation of one's natural beauty or hearing the music of one's soul (the bird in flight). The round shape of the conservatory also suggests the idea of a *temenos,* which in Greece was a small sacred place where one could find refuge and be safe from harm. It was an asylum wherein the Godhead was present. This concept is equally applicable here, for it provides a container for Leila's movement into a spiritual dimension.

The three women are presented with a problem and must coordinate their efforts. The talents of each are required to solve the problem of where to place two feathers that will enable the stone-like bird to fly. The feathers represent the bird (the part standing for the whole) which in this case perhaps can't fly because of the loss of essential "birdness." We refer to a situation where we feel stifled or caged by saying "our wings are clipped," as if to say one's spirit cannot fly. Among some native Americans it is a custom to attach feathers to articles in order to render them sacrosanct. The object, an aspect of the physical world, thus becomes an aspect of the spirit world. But in the dream this bird, magnificent as it is, has lost its ability to soar because it is hardened like a stone. It cannot fly because it lacks the necessary impetus for flight—the factors which endow it with sacredness have not been attached.

In previous dreams we spoke of various images of men as the animus, as spirit, but the white bird progresses beyond the human or personal element, the inner masculine, to a transpersonal level. The beautiful white bird symbolizes spirit, similar to the white dove that represents the Holy Spirit in religious paintings. The bird in the dream represents the transcendent function, the psychic dynamic which mediates opposites, but its flightlessness shows that this function is unable to move. Attitudes remain hardened and static.

The transcendent function facilitates a transition from one psychological attitude to another; it mediates between consciousness and the unconscious. However, when ego establishes itself as the center of the personality and does not cooperate with the Self, then the transcendent function is non-operative—stony and flightless. In many of the previous dreams, when a new image of the dark-haired woman appeared, causing the dreamer to run away, it was as if the transcendent function could not mediate between the unconscious and consciousness because of the rigid control by the dreamer's ego.

In the dream, the inflexibility of the ego is modified by recognizing what *is* needed as a launching device—the circular wire frame—a mandala or symbol of wholeness. Light and darkness, soma and psyche, masculine and feminine, consciousness and unconsciousness are all contained within this frame of wholeness. It is climbing and reaching with Logos, the masculine rational thinking function, that brings this possibility within reach.

Attaching the feathers is symbolic of assimilating new values by honoring the sacred aspects of one's being. If our concepts of spirit are projected only upward and outward—that is, unattached to our individual psychic life—then our lives become hardened like the stone bird. Attaching the feathers means redeeming that projection in order to integrate it as one's own, thus enabling a release of spirit. No longer encased in stone, the spirit can soar. Not only is there a release of Leila's imaging of the spiritual element within herself, but her perserverence to allow the spirit to take flight enables onlookers to join in as well. In the lysis of the dream, many birds are in flight. Apparently the release of personal spirit has a domino effect.

The image of the beautiful white bird is not unusual in dreams. Leila's bird was flightless; it had lost its ability to be a bird. In other people's dreams the white bird is starving or caught in a tree branch or has been wounded in some way. These incapacitated birds reflect the dreamer's personal situation, but they also indicate the condition of our collective consciousness: the woundedness of the world's spirit.

Leila

For days any semblance of hope for myself had been fading, but the dream of launching the stony dream bird excited me tremendously. I pondered the lesson of the myth I had first recalled at the sight of my mother's legs. Venus had turned to stone those women who spurned their bodies. I was confronted again by my own rigidity. There remained more for me to explore in the realm of the spirit. About the time of the dream, my insistent bouts of depression became less severe. I was a bit more at ease with others. It was indeed as if something stone-like had at last miraculously come to life within me. The white bird. Friends commented on the changes they saw in me, reflecting my new sense of confidence and vitality.

I began to pause at the beginning of each day, exactly as I had stood at the many doorways of the Metropolitan Museum, to let my invisible cord pull me forth. I imagined the dark-haired woman at the other end, drawing me to sit on the deck in the sunshine, eat a sandwich, telephone a friend or walk along the road to admire the wild flowers. I did not force myself to do anything, but waited for my body to carry me there. I allowed the mood of the moment to express itself. I was trusting my instincts, and this brought deep satisfaction. Also this invisible cord was helping me to establish a balance between my physicality and the symbolic world of my dreams, validating my choices. I no longer felt lost in the dark.

I discerned that the spirit was enlivening me. Of course this is looking back at the dream; it took me years to understand that the bird feathers were giving flight to my spirit, that gradually I was finding the celebration emphasized by the Virgin.

This celebration involved more than sexual passion, though it began there, as if that were indeed the launching pad of a mission toward awakening. The coming together of my sexuality and spirituality at last seemed possible.

21
Easter Eggs

There is a crowd of people at a formal dinner. I can see myself standing apart and alone. I wear a long heavy black gown with many golden rings on it. There is something different about me. I walk among the tables on the upper level of the large banquet hall and search for the place-card with my name. Men stand behind their chairs at the tables with vacant seats between them and wait for the women to be seated. Other women find their places, but there is no place-card for me. I go down to the lower level of the hall to an Easter-egg shop. A woman shows me beautiful large eggs that I can buy.

As in the dream of the shaman, we again find there is no place for Leila in this formal setting. Her name is not included among those to be seated. Her designated place seems to be somewhere other than in a social situation. There is an important moment of discernment when Leila realizes that there is something different about her, that she is an individual, no longer like others in the group

Leila's elegant black gown is embellished with gold rings. There is a noteworthy contrast between that and wearing "mother's clothes," as we saw in a much earlier dream, or even the tight satin outfit of the "femme fatale." There is a sense of stateliness in the figure. The gold rings that adorn the gown are analogous to the gold cross-stitched fabric in a previous dream, but instead of being hidden beneath the earth (in the unconscious), this asset is part of the conscious personality. The black gown with the gold rings, a symbol of the Self, indeed brings about a revisioning of oneself.

The gold rings also indicate an ego attitude in correct balance with the Self. Gold, a precious metal associated with the sun and solar consciousness, is symbolic of immortality and incorruptibility. Long-buried hidden treasures when redeemed from earth or watery graves are untarnished; therefore, gold can be thought of as eternal or related to the divine. It is in this sense we see the gold rings as symbolic of the Self.

Not finding her place in the milieu of collective consciousness, Leila descends to a deeper level. There she finds a shop to buy Easter eggs. The egg is life *in potentia*—completely contained, developing, but not yet ready to hatch. But these are special eggs, Easter eggs, which gives them greater importance. In ancient times, during the ritual spring celebrations honoring the earth goddess Astarte, eggs were colored with dyes made from herbs and earth. Then, as now, eggs carried the same symbolism as in Leila's dream—the promise of new life. In early Christianity, spring was the season to celebrate the risen Christ; many pagan customs from goddess worship and the rites of spring were carried over into Christian practices. In connection with colored eggs, our cultural myth maintains that the Easter Bunny brings them. This myth is also connected to ancient rites, for the rabbit is the animal of the Great Mother and is associated with fecundity.

The dream removes Leila from the collective mode of a formal social setting—an ambience of elegance and good manners—to a more profound level where she can connect with new life and the paradigm of fertility. This does not necessarily refer to physical fertility such as child-bearing, but to psychological fertility. This is not given to her nor does she simply find it; she must buy it. We normally think of money as a means of exchange, but it also connotes psychic energy, by which one is moved to obtain what is needed or desired.

Here we find Leila's psychic energy directing her to a deeper, more fertile field of development. It will cost her, not in terms of literal money but in the sense of concession. She must be willing to give up something belonging to an old sense of herself in order for new life to evolve. The ending of the dream does not tell us if Leila buys the egg, that is, if she relinquishes something in order to obtain the new life. We only know that it is available to her.

Leila

The morning after this dream my husband and I drove to visit my parents. To avoid conversation, not wanting to make the effort to leave the images from the night, I pretended to nap in the car. Half-way there we stopped at a restaurant and, as in the dream, when I saw myself in the restroom mirror I saw a difference, though there was no black gown with golden rings. My reflection reassured me of my capacity to relate to the man waiting in the car without asking his opinion on this or that. There was no need to "build him up," as my mother had taught. The woman emerging from within me could speak genuinely. The refugee was finally finding her voice. Smiling, I climbed in beside him to enjoy the rest of the ride.

I was encouraged that this experience contrasted so directly with the image of the clay mirror, where there was no reflection at all. I was making progress. To arrive at a dinner party with no card to show me my place at the table, even if it was only a minor lapse by a harried hostess, or perhaps my failure to reply to the invitation, had long been an anxiety of mine. Now, in my dream, I was living through it. My pervasive fear of being left out had to be more fully faced. I was terrified of being called on to celebrate alone.

Over the coming years I realized that I could stand on my own two feet and did not have to depend on the social world. Of course I often lost this sense of myself. Yearning to find my strength again, I would picture myself standing apart, golden rings hanging from my gown.

Continuing to catch myself in little lies that made up my persona, I doubled my attempts to listen to my thoughts and watch my move-ments. I could see through them better than when I was still shedding my mother's clothes, so to speak. Then I was always thinking, "How do I look to others?" I no longer needed to check. It was important for me to notice when I slipped back into old habits of relating, and I tried diligently to record each incident.

Also, I would have to give up needing a man to pull out my chair for me at meals. Likewise, I had to learn to walk through doors that my husband did not open. Understood metaphorically, these old ex-

pectations impeded my development. As with previous images I had worked with, this was exciting and at the same time threatening. I did not rely on my husband as heavily as in the past, but I had never considered complete independence, and it was astounding that my dream seemed to be insisting on it.

I became aware that when I entered a collective situation, such as a family gathering or a dinner party similar to the one in the dream, I reacted to it as if an aggregate "eye" turned my way to judge me.

Connecting the Easter eggs with new life, I remembered the rabbit I had made for my closet child and began to understand that my healing came from such instinctive actions. The urge to make the crude toy had risen spontaneously. Nonetheless, I was dismayed that I had to descend to an even lower level to achieve the new birth heralded by the eggs.

One morning, while cleaning the bathroom mirror, I caught sight of a dainty, graying, insecure female, nothing like the image of myself in the dream. As usual, after glimpsing myself as I might become, sooner or later the image evaporated, as if it had never surfaced, and only uncertainty remained. Doubts emerged with a vengeance. A powerful force pulled me toward my past. From mere shakiness I sank into despair, declaring to myself that it was all a distortion. The dark-haired woman had disappeared from my body, and reuniting with her was all that mattered.

22
The Dark-Haired Woman Returns

I visit a high-school friend's childhood house. I have a terrible time trying to bathe. First I can't get my clothes off, next there is no tub, then not enough water, then it is cold. So I return home, to Summer Wind. I prepare to bathe in my bathroom here, but it is now a larger and more opulent room. A short, dark-haired woman enters. We undress each other, pausing to embrace and to fondle each other's breasts. I touch the dark tufts of hair under her arms and we speak of our love for each other. As I step into the tub I notice a beautiful ointment jar on one end of the tub; on the label printed in large block letters is the word FRENCH. On the other end above the faucet is a majestic stand holding red soap shaped like a rose.

This dream recalls an image of a much earlier one, in which the dreamer meets a dark-haired girl and they explore each other's bodies. In that dream the two girls were to be married later, but not at that time because of the presence of the stern spinster figure symbolic of the severe mother complex then governing Leila's psychological life. In this dream we find a similar situation but with a completely different outcome. As if to paint a before-and-after picture, the dream sharply contrasts the attitudinal changes which have occurred.

With a schoolgirl's sensibility regarding sexuality, passion, love and relationships, cleansing oneself of old convictions appears impossible, as shown by the opening scene of the dream. And it is. One must "cleanse" that mind-set—all the entrenched injunctions and admonishments, originally taken in as unquestionable truths. The act of bathing is ridding oneself of accumulated dirt, refreshing and caring for the body. A hot soak in a tub relaxes tense muscles, soothes body and soul. As in the rite of baptism, in the dream water is used as a psychological cleanser to absolve one from stains upon the soul.

Realizing that cleansing cannot come about within the confines of the old belief systems, the dreamer moves to a place where it can. Psychic libido is directed away from adolescent attitudes to the place of the Summer Wind. How appropriate (and poetic) is the name of this new place in which to bathe. Wind, in religious and mythological thought, is symbolic of creative spirit. For example, the four winds were evoked by Ezekiel to bring life to the dry bones. We also find regenerative associations when recalling the miracle of Whitsun when like a wind the Holy Ghost filled the house.

Even prior to Christian writing, the sun god was thought to have a long tube connected to him like a phallus from which the procreative winds originated to disperse his fructifying rays. Many poets have used the metaphor of wind. In Coleridge's *The Ancient Mariner,* wind (or spirit) is the moving force opposing the stagnant calm. The driving energy of creative spirit opposes deadly inertia. The summer wind is not the harsh chilling winter wind, but a "cool and temperate wind of grace," as Shakespeare wrote in *Henry V.* It is in the house of the Summer Wind where Leila is to be washed in a moving and creative spirit. To reiterate, this does not necessarily mean creative in the sense of producing some external form of art, but is to be thought of in terms of living one's life as authentically as possible.

In the elegant bathroom where she once again meets the dark-haired woman, fully mature and no longer a girl, the appreciation of the beauty of the feminine being is realized. Leila demonstrates love for what was once degraded and repressed. This is an aspect of the cleansing process. In the opulent bathroom, as if to underscore the importance of this ritual cleansing, everything needed is there—the decorative jar of French ointments and the rose-shaped soap. Sensual pleasures such as food, wine, music, art—and certainly love and passion—are collectively associated with the French more than any other nationality. The dreamer's cleansing process will include a container for ointment labeled with the name symbolic of bodily pleasures.

The red rose is the flower of Aphrodite; the unfolding petals of the mature rose are evocative of woman's genitals. This image is also available for cleansing her personal misconceptions regarding her feminine nature, especially in regard to sensuality and sexuality. Luxuriating in the pleasures of bathing, as opposed to a hurried dip in the shower, rejuvenates body and soul. How quickly we forget the attention to body in our fast-paced world. The correlation of spirit and body is coming to the fore in Leila's awareness. Body needs spirit as spirit needs body. They give life to one another: the inspiriting of body and the embodiment of spirit.

There is another association with the dark-haired woman which I related to Leila. It is the image of the sacred prostitute, who epitomizes the integration of body and spirit. In ancient days when many gods and goddesses were worshipped, the sacred prostitute was the priestess in the temple dedicated to Aphrodite. In sacred precincts, the act of love-making was offered as a way of worship. The sacred prostitute sexually welcomed the world weary man as a way of bringing the loving gifts of the goddess into the soul of mankind. She infused instinctual sex with the ecstasy of love. Neither the act itself nor the priestess offering these gifts was considered dishonorable. Although we would have grave doubts today, then the priestess was seen as virtuous and the act of love-making sacred.

Women who were barren or who found no joy in sex and disdained their body also sought the blessing of Aphrodite through the sacred prostitute. She taught them the art of love-making, of caring for their bodies in order that they might feel beautiful, desired, receptive and loving. In this way the women who came to the sacred prostitute reverently worshipped the Goddess of Love.

The dark-haired woman who appears in the elegant bathroom possesses attributes similar to those of the sacred prostitute and serves a similar function. Her image carries aspects of the shadow element of Leila, as previously described, but she is more than repressed material of the personal unconscious. In association with the sacred prostitute, the dark-haired woman is also an archetypal image, the human embodiment of the Goddess of Love.

An archetype, an aspect of the collective unconscious, is a natural universal image, a portrait that gives form and direction to the instincts. When breaking through to consciousness, archetypal energy modifies or reconstructs conscious understanding. The structure of our belief system, once held as absolute truth, is altered not by willful choice but from the surging force deep within one's psyche moving in the direction of wholeness.

Leila

Upon waking, the image of the red-rose soap still with me, I bolted from the bed to the mirror. Again, my reflection seemed to have altered, and the damp washcloth on my skin felt sensuous. While brushing my teeth, I perceived the dark-haired woman's presence. After recording the dream I scribbled: "She reappears, and I am her lover!" I whispered my thanks for the fire running through my veins.

Recalling the wonderful dance that had taken me to the Milky Way, I swung my hips and enjoyed the vitality of my body. Since beginning analysis I had come a long way from the image of the starving woman in the mirror. Lounging in the tub, I frequently traced a fingertip along my curves to acknowledge the dark-haired woman. She truly lived in this body.

Often, when preparing to leave the house, an ache—that hurt, wounded feeling that we call homesickness—would come over me. Unable to continue dressing, I would cancel my plans. To avoid this, it was necessary to be aware of my dark lover choosing my outfit and sliding it on my body. Her disclosure of love echoed in my head, and I would then warm to myself and know my particular beauty. The ache would subside, and I would swish out the door. The pain of the child who could not face her life was healed.

If I forgot my dark-haired woman while making love to my husband, I lapsed into pretending to be a Playboy centerfold, with my hair a shining mass, breasts perfect, legs slender and shapely. In the past, this had carried me through my wifely duties, but I was ready to forsake the falsehood that prevented me from treasuring my own flesh. Now I reveled in the freedom of my body's movements. My dark-haired woman was becoming an engaging playmate, and I was developing a fierce dedication to be who she encouraged me to be.

Standing in a crowd at a party, unhappy at being left out, I sorted out that my discomfort came not because of alienation from the people there, but from the dark-haired woman. With the memory of her fondling on my skin, I was more relaxed and responsive to others.

I constantly oriented myself with my refugee-declaration two years earlier: "I don't know where I'm going, only that I must go." By exploring my dreams, determined to deal with whatever surfaced, I was steadily filling the empty human shell.

That spring my mother died. I fortified myself with a bright skirt and purple sash, the very color she had considered "common." Nevertheless, anxiety consumed me as I took part in the funeral rituals. I wanted to be agreeable to my family, but my dark-haired warmth was blocked and I could only imitate a kind and sociable person in a mechanical way.

23
The Dark-Haired Woman Is My Therapist

My therapist is a beautiful dark-haired woman. She wears flowing silk pants and her shiny hair swings about her shoulders. She takes me to her new office in a faraway city. A little girl with pigtails and freckles, full of fun, joins our session. The therapist lets her stay if she'll be quiet, but of course she isn't. The little girl sees a dirty rubber bag with an attached hose and asks the therapist what it is. The therapist says that it is an enema bag. She fills it with water and walks toward me with it. She says, "Yes, certain people in your life say that you have to take it." I knock the bag out of her hand, and yell, "No, I will not!" The therapist claps her hands, "Good for you!" she says.

The months following Leila's mother's death were conflictual, as one can imagine.

Caught between mutually antagonistic emotions of relief that her ill and aged mother was no longer a presence in her life, and the grief of knowing that her conflict with her mother could never be resolved, Leila experienced a time of darkness and despair. Watching the final breath leave her mother's body and seeing her coffin covered with dirt did not bring release from her inner struggle: loving the woman who had given her life and yet hating her for destroying the very substance of that life. She was "unmothered." Once again, the desperation of her soulful child, like the closet child, was ushered to the forefront of consciousness.

We observe the circuitous way of psyche's healing, working first with one split-off aspect and then another that leap-frogs to the head of the line. One seems to be retracing old material, images which have long since been laid to rest—or so we thought. Each time a complex is constellated—usually by an external event—we are faced with psychic reflection and the emotions associated with it. In a spiraling manner, we are faced with the image and feel the affect but each time in a more profound way. The cleansing bath redeemed aspects of Leila's feminine nature, her sexuality, but other traumas, perhaps more severe, had to be consciously understood and dealt with. The image this dream brought to consciousness was an enema bag and all that symbolized for Leila.

The dream therapist, her internalized therapist, presents a figure of a woman unrestricted and flowing. The looseness of her clothes and hair suggest her ability to allow the natural chain of events to occur, as a river finds its natural direction. The flow is downward and deepening as the therapist takes Leila to a new place within, far away from conscious thought. She allows the playful child, the natural child, to be present, for she is necessary to the therapeutic situation. It is fitting that it is the child who first spots the enema bag and questions its use, for this was an item symbolic of the wounds inflicted upon the spirited child.

Upon reflection, Leila saw the hot enemas her mother determinedly administered as a rape. Indeed it was a rape of the psychic life of the child. Not only the physical invasion of some hard foreign object but the woundedness inflicted by mother on daughter in many hurtful experiences was a psychological rape that the enema bag came to symbolize.

In knocking the enema bag aside, the dreamer is protecting the development of the inner child, thus becoming good mother to herself.

Leila

The dark-haired therapist appeared a few weeks after my mother's death, when my mind was almost constantly battered with "dead-Mom" thoughts, as I now understood them. "From beyond the grave" had taken on an added, ominous meaning.

I wept, not with grief, but with fury at the negativity I had carried from her into my own life. My unyielding words, to myself and others, about the terrible mother she had been, rang in my ears. She truly lived on within me.

The dream forced a memory when I hoped to put my girlhood as far behind me as possible. From the onset of menstruation, my mother administered hot enemas to relieve my cramping. She filled an ugly red rubber bag (exactly as it materialized in the dream) with close to boiling water and hung it from the shower curtain rod, then sat in a chair beside the tub. Stressing that it was what her mother had done for her, she made me lean across her lap while she inserted the nozzle, urgent in her demands to hold still and take more water. I always cried, pleading for her to stop. She held me down firmly, promising that it would ease my pain. Until I left for college, whenever I had my period, the enemas were a part of my life. Reliving the scene, I realized that I had indeed experienced a kind of rape, and, too compliant to scream, my insides had absorbed the rage.

Grateful for the dream's gift of the fun-loving child, over the following months I kept her image near. I bought us brightly colored pens, took piano lessons and snuggled my Dalmatian puppy in bed. Once, on the sidewalk en route to a concert, I twirled to let my new cotton skirt swish around my legs, and suddenly knew that my child's gaiety and my woman's dancing joy were close companions. Whenever I heard the telltale tone in my voice beseeching approval (an ingrained tendency so difficult to overcome), I let my little gal say something ridiculous.

This sense of play began to permeate my days, and my marriage, which I considered to be my second, albeit to the same man, was stronger. After enjoying him, I would sometimes dance in a circle to thank the dark-haired woman for sweetening the air between us.

There were many more years of work before dead-Mom thoughts no longer bothered me, before I could allow myself to trust whatever emotion came, whether confusion or anger or fear or even contentedness. I was cautious not to fall into seeking the approval of others and became impatient with myself when I did, forgetting the difficulty of breaking this habitual conduct. My little red-haired dynamo helped. She was becoming increasingly precious to me, and sometimes I imagined that she was a buddy to my closet child, Ann. When talking to them, I often felt the familiar judgment of "crazy," yet the changes

I saw in myself served to override that objection.

My growing passion for life seemed to affirm me, and I began to relish being in my own presence. Yet persistent doubts about how I was spending my time plagued me ("Nothing but selfish, Leila, caring only for yourself with all this self-examination . . . ").

24
A Foul Thing

I see him, but I cannot see myself. He is a dwarf-man who lives in the hold of a ship. I watch him come and go. He scampers about on his short legs and careens from side to side like the ship itself. He is a foul thing. I'm not sure that others know about him, but I know that he murders and steals in order to live. Hanging in his hold is a dead body without arms and only red holes where the eyes once were. The dwarf-man pushes the body aside as if it were a curtain.

This dream reminded me of a novelette entitled *The Dwarf,* by Par Lägerkvist, a Swedish Nobel prize winner in literature. The story tells of a kingdom ruled by a kind and compassionate king who had a loving wife and daughter. The kingdom was peaceful, the people healthy and happy, and the land prosperous.

Among the king's retinue was a jester, a dwarf who entertained the court, and when serious situations arose he acted the fool so others would not forget humor. There is no situation, however serious, that doesn't contain a slice of the ridiculous, and the clever dwarf exemplified this with his amusing antics.

The king, becoming more and more dependent on the jester-dwarf, projected onto him attributes of wisdom and trustworthiness; consequently the dwarf became more empowered. He stood behind the throne and whispered in his sire's ear. Soon the king's thoughts and words were only those of the dwarf.

Not content with having exclusive access to the king, the dwarf wanted more power; he wanted to wear the crown and rule the kingdom. He plotted exactly how to do this by first destroying all that was feminine, starting with the princess's cats, then the princess herself. Finally, he spun a web of madness which enveloped the queen. Without the feminine ruling principle, that is without Eros, the king be-

came hard and embittered, ruling with an iron fist, declaring war on
other kingdoms and making judgments without mercy—all at the
urging of the jester. As one would expect, ruin, famine and a plague
swept the land. The once fertile kingdom lay in waste.

Leila's dream presents a similar picture. The dwarf, the imprisoning
negative animus image which we first met under the cathedral, is now
in command in the bowels of the ship. The structure of a cathedral
and that of a ship are not unrelated. In Latin the word *nave* means
ship and came to be used also as the nave of a cathedral, whose lofty
ceiling, constructed with supporting spine and ribs, is built like the inverted hull of a ship. One is raised toward the heavens while the other
sails the deep waters of the unconscious.

We speak of Christ as being the "Captain of my ship" or of the
Church as the vessel of Christianity. In opposition, or in inverted
fashion, this malevolent dwarf embodies the dark side of Christianity.
In the decorative sculpture of medieval and Renaissance cathedrals,
such as the Sistine Chapel or the Baptistery in Florence, we find the
dark side of religious observance depicted in dwarf-like forms combining human and animal features, both as tempter of the living and
torturer of the damned. He sows disunity and inspires hatred. He destroys compassion and relatedness to self and others.

Stormy seas, stormy unconscious. No clear sailing. Leila's center
does not hold. The dreamer says, "I cannot see myself." Literally,
Leila has lost sight of her core being, thus opening the door for the
demon-like images that spring from the unconscious. In the dream
this loathsome figure is not only in control but is on a murderous
rampage. He murders the essence of being by stealing soul, leaving one
with an armless body that cannot embrace and empty eye-sockets
that cannot envision the future. This is a graphic image of what remains when a malevolent animus is in control.

In the course of analysis and deep introspection, distrust of oneself
often surfaces. What is the purpose of this crazy-making process, so
expensive in time, energy and money? One feels a loss and at a loss.
Doubt is not unexpected and not without purpose. Periods of disbelief

and doubt belong to the psychological process of enantiodromia, a principle which holds that at some point everything turns into its opposite. When everything is seemingly rosy and one is at one's best, up pops the devil! He torments self-assurance with relentless badgering, questions such as: if you are developing as you think yourself to be, why aren't you happier or more content? Why the endless struggle? Give it up! If we succumb to such edicts, he indeed destroys our soul.

The images of this dream are more than personal; that is, they do not belong only to Leila's individual psychology. As archetypal dreams often do, this dream also represents a view of the world's psychology—the collective state of unconsciousness. If an extreme one-sided tendency is held uppermost in consciousness, then inevitably the reverse will happen. The law of enantiodromia will come into effect. The lofty vision of Christianity today fails to see what the Renaissance painters knew so well. It fails to take into account the reverse side of its lofty structures—the dark hold of its own ship. The foul little murderous creature is more than a personal demon, he is objective evil intent on destroying the *anima mundi*, the world's soul.

Jung writes,

> The only person who escapes the grim law of enantiodromia is the man who knows how to separate himself from the unconscious, not by repressing it—for then it simply attacks him from the rear—but by putting it clearly before him as *that which he is not*.[15]

This statement, it seems to me, shows the crucial importance of becoming aware of one's unconscious dark side. Individuation comes about by seeing into the darkness of our personal life as well as our collective life, acknowledging the very real malevolent factors and thereby making them conscious. When light and dark, the opposites, are in correct balance, enantiodromia does not occur.

Leila

This dream came when my husband and I had driven out of state for

---

[15] *Two Essays on Analytical Psychology,* CW 7, par. 112.

a greatly anticipated weekend. Disappointed with my nervousness, I had believed that once away from my frustrations at home I would be able to relax and my dark-haired self so recently enjoyed would emerge. Something quite different happened.

Horrified, I opened my eyes to the frilly room in the inn, sickened that this foul thing—the dwarf—still found sustenance in me. Denunciations of self washed through me. How was I to get through the day, much less the weekend? My limbs rigid, I made it through our candlelight dinners. Listening with longing to the laughter of the other couples, I realized that the dwarf had stolen my sense of fun.

Back home, my mind was preoccupied for weeks with the foul dwarf. I pondered my mother's constant reaction to my girlhood enthusiasm: "Too full of yourself. You need to be sawed off at the knees!" Gradually, I realized that she had introduced me to the loathsome creature, instilling in me at an early age that it was wrong to enjoy life.

A year later I had another dream in which the dwarf told me that his name was Critical Spirit. At that time I understood that the poison he had left in me had seeped into my environment. I was passing on what I had suffered from my mother. Again the question was: how to stop doing so?

The answer presented itself in a rather mundane way. Running errands one afternoon, on impulse I bought my husband a bottle of cologne, intending to hide it for the next gift-giving occasion. That evening an argument erupted, and any semblance of relatedness evaporated as my acid tongue took over. I told myself to lighten up. Reaching for a newspaper, I playfully tapped him before rushing to retrieve the cologne to spray his neck and sniff out the spots to kiss. My fun-loving child had saved the day. When I was aware of her presence, my haughty attitude slid away. Her spunk could keep me from letting the dwarf have his way with me.

I recorded other instances of my enthusiasm in my journal, developing eyes that could see the healing, and faith in myself to take responsibility. I was careful to move more like a frolicsome kitten than a cross old cat. I monitored my body for stiffening, because if ignored, my limbs reflected the hardening of my heart. Bit by bit I learned to stop my pretenses and concentrate on fashioning myself into a larger container for my dark-haired warmth.

Years earlier, when beginning analysis, I had recognized my lack of vitality, as if a victim of a holocaust. Now I saw more clearly the truth of my body hanging with no arms or eyes in the ship's hold. I heard Scott Peck point out in a lecture that evil is "live" spelled backward. I agreed.

Though this negativity thrived in me, as it had in my mother, my trust in my dreams enabled me finally to respond to it. The natural child's spirit was being restored. I was filled with hope. The dark-haired woman had given me new eyes with which to view myself, and I could not let the despicable dwarf jab them out. It was literally years before I was no longer intermittently snagged by him, but the image in the previous dream of the black-haired therapist who could allow my little imp to speak was the antidote to his poison.

25
Brightly Colored Tadpoles

I buy four little black puppies to give to the others that I live with. When I get them home and realize that I have to care for them I become pretty unhappy—they mess everywhere and do not stay still. I also buy four tadpoles and put them in a large round glass table-bowl with a glass cover. My companions and I discuss whether or not they will be able to live with such a tight cover. Our prior sex therapist calls to ask how my husband and I are doing. I assure her that we are doing fine, but she appears and hangs around as if to check on me.

Next I shop for a mirror. There is one in a pretty frame that I consider, but even though the others encourage me to buy it I refuse, saying that I cannot see myself clearly because it has strips of metal across it in a waffle pattern. I decide to return the wriggly pups to the shop and forfeit my money. But the tadpoles stay. As I watch them swim about they seem to change before my very eyes into beautiful colors that become brighter and brighter.

"Happiness is a warm puppy." That was Leila's spontaneous response when asked for her association to puppies. Indeed they bring to mind images of playful, cuddly balls of fur who generously offer little puppy kisses when held close to the face. Unless ill treated, they may be imagined as the epitome of unconditional love, for they react to all humans in a similar manner. To be responded to by another with the same delight as one finds with a puppy is happiness, for it warms the heart. Warm puppy attributes are a gift of Eros we may give to others, or receive from them. However, in the dream Leila finds caring for the puppies a messy business, time consuming and too much of a bother. Instead, she is enraptured with the tadpoles.

A tadpole is the early stage of an amphibian. Schoolchildren learn the marvels of nature by observing the metamorphous of this minute, wriggly creature as it develops into a frog in clearly distinguishable stages. The tadpole's shape, a large head propelled by a tail, is not unlike that of sperm, the masculine fertilizing factor. This is what Leila finds so fascinating. The germ of the creative masculine component, colorful and dynamic, remains in a primitive state of development, swimming in the waters of the unconscious.

The tadpoles in the dream are encased in a tightly sealed glass container, not in their natural habitat. This image suggests that this unconscious component continues to be insulated from feelings, like a subject in a laboratory. A research scientist becomes enthused about a project, fascinated by studying it, but stays emotionally detached, unaware of the effect the observation of the object has on the observer. Although enraptured by the colorful tadpoles, Leila did not feel their stirring movements inwardly. As this is an early larva stage of development, their transformation still incomplete, presumably it is too soon for more than observation.

Why tadpoles and not, for instance, a sprouting seed? This leads us to ask what this psychic aspect is that is in an early stage of transformation and moving toward maturity. In the case of a tadpole, it develops into a frog or a toad, and so in addition to the symbolism of the tadpole, we must look at the symbol of the frog.

The frog is amphibious, living both in water and on dry land. Its meaning is ambiguous. In folklore frogs are often associated with witches or the devil—as a main ingredient of the poisonous brew they concoct. On the other hand, parts of frogs were also used as an aphrodisiac or love charm. We hear the cacophony of croaking frogs in springtime, a season when nature is budding and thoughts of love and sexual desire come to the fore. Like the sporadic leaping of frogs, unconscious complexes leap spontaneously into consciousness to bedevil us. This is why, in the dream, the sex therapist is calling. A phone bell or door bell or church bell awakens or alerts us to some message. Not content with Leila's remark that everything is "fine," the therapist remains connected as if something is left unsaid.

Leila continues to seek her own image. Whereas the mirror she finds in the shop more clearly defines the vision of herself than did the clay mirror in a previous dream, it is superimposed with metal bands. We are unsure just what kind of metal, but other than copper, the metal of Venus, metal is related to gods: Saturn, lead; Jupiter, tin; Mars, iron. We could say that at this time her feminine nature is overlaid with constrictive bands, not unlike the harsh, dictatorial rule of Saturn.

We look at the symbols of the puppies, the tadpoles/frogs and the metal-banded mirror and how they weave together. In the dream, Leila found the puppies too messy to deal with and returned them to the shop, though she knew it would cost her. She is unable to receive, that is, be "refunded" in the giving or receiving of Eros or happiness which the warm puppies represent. She remains content to watch the cold-blooded components swimming in the unconscious—not on a feeling level, but observing—thinking about them in a mechanical way. Metamorphosis of tadpoles into frogs is indicated, but it is an open question whether the frogs are used by the witch or are symbolic of love and fertility.

As a result of negating Eros and becoming enraptured by unconscious material, Leila's feminine nature, the image of herself, is bound to judgments or logic, the patriarchal world. In the diligent search to find herself, she is losing a connection to others in her life and to outer reality. We do not individuate by deep introspection alone; we must also bring our insights into daily life and our interactions with others. Both are important and must be maintained simultaneously. The task is arduous and ongoing.

Leila

The tadpoles versus the pups heralded a monumental inner battle. Nancy cautioned me about overdoing introspection, suggesting that perhaps this dream warned of my submersion in the unconscious drama. She assured me that she was not pushing me toward popularity like my mother had, but was concerned with balance. Nonetheless, since "outer," for me, had become synonymous with "popular," I heard her as my mother ordering me to become more extraverted.

Determined to no longer follow my dead mother's directions, I became angry. I later understood that when anyone invited me out for fun, I tended to react to the hated maternal manipulation.

In the meantime I was terribly confused. Despite the trouble I was having with practical details, I wanted to stay with the splendor of my inner process, the glorious ever-varying colors of the tadpoles floating around my head. It seemed to me that to forsake them would negate my awe of the unfolding mystery story. After all, I had made progress by carefully monitoring the inner changes. In my scheme of things, it was either the tadpoles or the puppies. One had to go. I did not know how to let the beauty and strength of both live in me.

Afraid of losing the link to my depths by being too realistic, and at the same time suspecting that a large part of me had never wanted to deal with the nitty-gritties of daily survival (and had maneuvered others into doing this for me), I resisted, getting nowhere. Difficult to face was my own laziness. Being flighty and irresponsible was my unconscious way of hooking others into taking care of me.

As for the wriggly pups, I just did not know how to bring them into my life, because often when I tried to play around, showing a lighter side of my personality, I fell right into what I considered my princess silliness. This didn't feel real like a warm puppy, but superficial.

Around the time of the dream about my black-haired therapist, I had been thankful for the fun-loving child who could dare to speak up and be ridiculous, risking the censure of others and myself. I had loosened up a good bit. Now I was afraid to allow myself to continue playing. Falseness I dreaded most, and my princess was certainly that, negating the dark-haired woman. Or so I thought.

I was indeed celebrating the mystery of my inner life by approaching my dreams with the thrill of expectancy. How to bring this excitement out into the sensate world?

In the midst of the struggle, the following dream disclosed an imminent danger.

26
Afraid for Her Life

(I awakened in the middle of the night with a throbbing head and wrote the following. It was as if I were writing and awakened while writing this and so was continuing to write.) I stood by her hospital bed and watched her dark sleeping head. I reached my hand under the cover to find her pulse and felt its weakness. Then I left her to seek help. The nurse and three orderlies were on their lunch-break. I told them her story. The orderlies were immediately interested, but only when I told abut her weak pulse was the nurse's interest piqued. Suddenly, inexplicably, I was afraid for Madame, afraid for her life, that is.

This dream followed the puppies/tadpole dream by several days. After returning the puppies and staying intent on examining the tadpoles, that is, concentrating on the inner life while neglecting outer relationships, it is not surprising to find the dark-haired woman in a near moribund condition. The vital fluid of life streaming through the body and psyche is weakening, as is the healthy connection with what the dark-haired woman symbolizes: feminine sexuality and spirituality.

The dream literally awakens Leila to this fact. With the nurses and orderlies she is able to obtain help. These self-regulating psychic components offer care and order. Leila refers to the woman in the bed as Madame. Not only is this a title for a married woman, it is also a title of distinction, as one would address royalty. On the other hand, "Madame" may refer to the manager of a brothel, a not inappropriate association considering the sexual energy she had come to represent for Leila, as sacred prostitute.[16] In the act of naming, the dark-haired woman is titled or "entitled" to a value. Although in a perilous state, the image of the dark-haired woman is becoming a ruling aspect of Leila's consciousness.

---

[16] See above, p. 120.

In another dream a few nights later there was an image of Leila on the floor, her legs unable to support her. With great difficulty she crawls to an object whereby she can pull herself up to a standing position. Painstakingly, Leila is nursing herself back to life, finding order in the relationship between inner and outer reality, a new stance.

Leila

The dark-haired woman's weak pulse truly frightened me, and I barely held desperation at bay. Other losses I might have survived, but not her riches. If she died, I would be left knowing myself as the invalid-princess, unable to relate warmly to family and friends. I was betraying my inner woman, yet I could not understand how. Guilt paralyzed me for some time.

I recalled that the dark-haired woman, as dream therapist, had invited my mischievous child to stay with us, letting her speak out. This told me that I needed to encourage this little girl, letting her continue to help me as she had from time to time through the previous months. Yet I constantly feared making a fool of myself. As in sex therapy two years earlier (this counselor had indeed appeared along with the tadpoles and pups), I persevered, electing to work with what I had, not with what I wished I had. I dared not neglect the dark-haired woman's weak pulse. I realized that it was not the princess who canceled my vitality, but my laziness. I confronted it and made the effort.

Alone in the house, I danced as freely as I could, picturing my child's red pigtails swinging through the air as I twirled. I took this little girl outside to run and laugh at my Dalmatian's antics. I stepped from my bath and rubbed lotion on my body, conscious of trying to revive the woman-beneath-my-skin, my dark-haired woman.

Gradually, I saw through my ploy as a wish to escape my everyday endeavors, which, compared to the beauty of the dream images, seemed mundane indeed. The surprise was that when I related to others with my dark-haired self, enthusiasm throbbed through my body, and my activities didn't feel in the least bit mundane.

Over time I learned to relax more and to throw back my head to let my laughter come from my gut, expressing my joy through a natural celebration, not at all like the princess's silliness.

The refrain of "Ave Maria" sometimes sang in my head, reminding me of the Virgin's exhortation to celebrate my life. Keenly aware of a mysterious inner support, I began to relish the adventure of my days, treasuring times when a spark appeared between myself and another person. I interrupted my usual litany of complaints, thankful for my awakening, determined to keep the woman-beneath-my-skin in sight.

Initiating my own plans sustained this inner woman, and when I murmured to my hips, "Swing out there," courage to be her/myself came. Warmth rose from my female core, and my reflection in the mirror showed me, once again, that the woman who mattered was within. Through the years I learned to be responsible for her life.

27
The Same Ego

I am excited, planning on going somewhere, and it will soon be time to bathe in preparation. I stand outside the house where I now live on the ground floor. The floor is smooth earth. There is a small patch of concrete inside where I park my car. I realize that I am the same ego whether in my dream life or in waking life and I will soon step over into my waking life.

In figuratively pulling herself up and standing on her own two feet, Leila once again came in touch with the dark-haired woman. Her enlivened spirit brought harmony and a sense of wholeness. The dream confirms this impression as it complements the ego's position.

"Planning on going somewhere" suggests movement to the next phase of growth and conscious understanding. And that does bring excitement. Bathing is a necessary preparation. Again we find the cleansing bath as ritual—removing stains and "dirt" in order not to carry the old attitudes into a new beginning.

The place where Leila now resides is well grounded, her feet on solid earth. She stands firm, not soaring to the heavens or underground, nor is she hypnotized by psychic contents swimming in the unconscious. Her car is readily accessible, meaning that the necessary libido is available for the coming change. Leila's insight that she is the same in dream reality as in actual existence is a dramatic understanding. She is able to resolve the complexity of valuing both inner and outer worlds simultaneously. She can move in or out and her ego remains unaltered.

Whereas the ego is something less than the total personality, it is responsive to demands of the Self. As the center of consciousness, the ego functions to maintain the total personality when balancing outgoing conscious connections and reflecting on material from the unconscious. The balance provides the ability to move in or out. Through her concerted efforts to pull herself up, Leila gained a well-grounded ego. No longer mesmerized by her unconscious life, she is able to maintain a proper psychic balance.

Leila

I wakened, and as my feet hit the floor I knew I was stepping over into the morning, exactly as the dream had stated. I wept with relief at being able to stay with my dream life, and the sense of myself I was discovering there, while going about my daily affairs. My soul's ego and my body's were in essence the same. Finally, I could begin to live in both places. My dream ego was the "as if" of metaphor, but it became actuality when I worked with it. The dream ego stood behind me, but the effort to bring myself out into the world was mine.

This dream somehow reawakened me to the gifts of the dreams. I browsed back through them, gaining a deeper understanding of the images and grounding them in my life as they transformed my misconceptions about myself.

The rat, I no longer feared. My mother's clothes, I no longer wore to cover the empty shell I once was. My child has broken out of the closet, though I still carried her despair, careful to tend to the small girl who imitated others instead of enjoying what she herself liked. I know that the loss of this metaphorical child had been fully as tragic, for me, as the loss of a flesh and blood one would have been. The tiger and space man juices I began to welcome. The wheel chair was destroyed, and though Princess No-Face had chosen my partner, my new self had saved the day. My marriage grew increasingly stronger. The snake in the pot was a symbol I repeatedly thrilled to, and the clay mirror was formed anew. The garden of innocence was left behind, alive in my memory, but without its hold on me. I was growing ever more comfortable with myself as a refugee escaping my collective mentality to find safety and well-being within myself.

In a recent dream my friend Paul, handsome in a red sweater, came to dance with me, my gigolo god alive in my heart. I no longer identified with the femme fatale. By staying alive to the various facets of my femininity, I do not as readily use it for seduction. I understand that my sex appeal has little to do with my outer appearance, but with the desire to love emanating from my body. My gratitude to the Virgin Goddess named Mary lives on, and I now appreciate that she supported my sexuality because she supported my life.

I have moved from screaming No to my overwhelming negative mother complex to saying Yes to myself. The secret of my gold crosses is forever close, as is the Milky Way. The enlivening of the stony white bird, the real meaning of Easter eggs, the significance of both tadpoles and puppies, the dearness of my free-spirited natural child, I keep them all in mind. And the foul thing within me no longer murders my enthusiasm. For I have learned that as disturbing as such images can be, I must stay aware of the character of each and forgive their transgressions.

I am a different person from the one who first consulted her dreams because, most vitally, the dark-haired woman's blood flows through my veins, bringing me a sense of my own warmth.

28
A Birthday Celebration

Nancy and I sit and eat at a small round table. Then several women and I paint a house a bright yellow-orange and I stand back to view it. I declare loudly that I really like it. Later we observe the dark-haired woman's first birthday. I go upstairs and find her lounging on a pad in the corner of her room. She is a large beautiful woman with long black hair. She lies on her side, nude, but partially covered with a crimson cloth tied around her hair and flowing freely down her body. I bring her downstairs for the celebration.

The round table denotes equality and collegiality, as in the Arthurian legend. There is no leader's position; it is continuous, a symbol of wholeness like a mandala. Analyst and analysand have entered a new relationship, with each having equal authority. It is as if the new beginning can be honored by breaking bread together. Not only is this true in the analytic relationship, it is true in terms of her locus of inner authority. She is one unto herself.

The house, symbolizing her psychic space, is painted bright yellow-orange. The dream does not say if this is Leila's place of residence but it is quite likely so. Yellow-orange is the color of the sun, symbol of solar consciousness. With the new-found conscious understanding that she has the same ego within as without, the inner light shines out like the sun's fructifying rays.

The image of the dark-haired woman reclining on a cushion is reminiscent of Goya's painting, *The Naked Maja*, splendid in her comfortable repose and beautiful in her nudity. The same could be said for Leila's image of her inner dark-haired woman. The crimson drape suggests a combination of red and blue—red being the color of passion and blue symbolic of spirit. The passions of spirit and body are united. Crimson, like the color purple, is a sign of royalty. The entitlement of "Madame" has bestowed a higher authority on her image as the feminine component of the archetype of the Self. Together, Leila and the dark-haired woman descend the stairs to commence the birthday celebration.

Recall the mystery story dream in the introduction, where Leila takes a live yet gasping fish from the invalid maiden and brings it down the stairs, out into her night-sea journey. Here, once again, she descends the stairs hand-in-hand with the symbol of revitalized feminine nature, the dark-haired woman. She is the core of Leila's personhood. Indeed something to be celebrated! Leila's vow to the Virgin Mary, "I will serve you by celebrating *my life,*" is now realized. New life is born, embracing the broad range of emotions—joy and pain, suffering and serenity, passion and pleasure, beauty and ugliness. Leila lives her life.

Leila's Epilogue

During these years, from within depression, many instances of grace have come through the steadfastness of the dark-haired woman. Never did she falter in showing me the way, only I in perceiving it. Picturing the crimson cloth from the birthday celebration flowing over my body, I knew that her vitality was mine. The passion in my very bones attested to her presence. I had brought her into my reality, and she blessed my laughter. Making a toast with my husband, I murmured beneath my breath, "Happy birthday, Leila."

Engaging in ordinary activities, I recognized that to refuse to embrace my commonness was to be ungrounded. I more easily connected with family and friends, aware that my need to relate authentically far outstripped the shame of my emotions. Less upset by the negative ones, I admitted them to myself instead of stuffing them down in an attempt to be a "good" person. The aftermath of this, always a surprise to me, was that I could often choose to be kinder to others.

It has taken decades to confront myself, but there could be no transformation until this was accomplished. The moral judgments that isolated me from myself and others had to be suspended. I began to appreciate the tenacity of my search, fueled by desperation. I have been privileged to watch myself unfold as princess, princess-wife, woman-with-the-rosy-claws, and then the dark-haired woman. Truly, I am fortunate to have attended this evolution.

When writing this epilogue, I found myself in the clutches of the negative mother complex. Though I knew that by telling my story I was living my soul's destiny, the venomous complex urged me to deny my interaction with the unconscious aspects of myself and my resulting transformation.

Being stuck in the complex has been like having both feet mired in mud, paralyzed and cut off from my creative resources. In analysis I

*have worked and worked and pulled and pulled, separating myself
with one last tug, only to look down at the muck clinging to my toes.
Yet having learned to virtually stand outside myself to observe the effect of this annihilating energy has allowed me to resist the complex
and to scrape away at the residue.*

*My psyche was wounded to such a degree that my thoughts and
feelings were motivated by an all-consuming guilt that tarnished everything. Of course complete freedom is beyond my scope, but the invisible circle first imagined years ago has embedded itself in my soul
to shield me from the censures. Recently I have laughed at anecdotes
family members recited about my mother, able to admire the positive
features of her personality. And amazingly, she has visited my dreams
to lend me her support.*

*Holding my past within, I dwelled on various levels at the same
time, an eye toward the messages gleaned from my dreams. Constantly heedful of witnessing myself as they portrayed me, I forsook
the limited view of my ego. Jungian psychology had not confined me
by focusing on a diagnosis, and for this I was thankful. When former
attitudes about myself sneaked in, the all-encompassing directive of
the Virgin to consecrate my life, as it gradually revealed itself, restored my reality, that which I had failed to grasp in my reach for the
ideal.*

*Whatever I was doing, whether walking my Dalmatian, playing the
piano, or opening my door to greet a friend, I reminded myself to
take pleasure in it as a mini-celebration, blocking my judgment of
how it appeared to others.*

*When depressed or anxious, I worried that the celebration had
evaporated, but came to realize that diligent observation of myself,
though not exactly happy-go-lucky, is a form of joy-making. I tried to
stay with the sense of my particular reality, ready to be corrected by
the unconscious when making mistakes.*

*Nine years after this birthday dream, further encouragement came
with the following dream:*

My Virginal Self

I leave my mother's bed to climb into a woman's car. Her vulva is the most beautiful I've ever seen. A rose in various stages can be seen through a round hole with a smaller hole above it. Smooth, soft skin surrounds both openings. Drawing back, I exclaim, "You're a virgin!" Pulling me close, she calmly replies, "I am your virginal self." We make love.

As the days pass I am increasingly at one with myself. Is this really me? I pinch my flesh. From the mirror, I peer back with ever clearer eyes. Finally, I understand that because of my psychological virginity I will usually stay in harmony with myself. Once I equated feminine beauty with conventional goodness and purity—in a word, righteousness—but my dreams have taught me that the woman within is the true embodiment of radiance. She recognizes herself, never requiring the compliments of others. At times I marvel at the joy of being alive, far from the days of dread. This joy seems to have a life of its own, which I welcome. I have found my voice, and it often rings with enthusiasm.

The circumstances in my outer life remain pretty much the same, and the wonder is that I do not desire to alter them. Yet my assorted roles smother me if I lose sight of my psyche's capacity for change. Although my tête-à-tête with my dreams engenders confidence, it throws me into anxiety when I cleave to the past instead of listening to the demands for metamorphosis.

With my newly found self-assurance, I try to display an appropriate face for each situation. Keeping in mind the reality of my individuation process, I dress comfortably and hold my uncertainties within. Not long ago I actually liked my persona when at a party.

I am beginning my third marriage, still to the same man, whose company I like. I do not know what to expect. With my growing faith in myself I will meet whatever challenges arise and can only hope not to hinder my husband's journey to himself.

With comprehension of my psychological setup, I am aware of my strengths. I am "making it." As with most significant realizations, it now seems simple, yet the years of getting here were anything but.

Discovering that my feminine self has an inherent spirituality has disrupted the status quo of my immediate community, to which I had tightly adhered in the past. To learn to live fervently by revelations from the unconscious, bowing with respect to the rules of my culture, has been a hard lesson. It all depends on knowledge of myself as an individual. The core of my being contains the seeds of my health, which I now understand as the ability to be myself. When disconnected from this center—and the tip-off is that I cannot hear what I call my woman's music reverberating through my body—I imagine diving down within, then dancing forward from that point, once more in tune with my inborn flow.

Through the spiritual discipline of analysis, my journey was begun. Though having left organized religion, I find that waiting to see what comes up from within myself before acting is a deeply religious way to lead my life.

I continue to spend time deciphering my dreams. Paying close attention to them has brought the uncanny perception that they shape my life. I am a living, breathing self, all the while being stitched from the unconscious. This dream-vigil is my supreme value, to which I return again and again to discern the personal vocabulary I can trust. I can rely on my alliance with my dreams, and it has come to be as integral a part of my days as any other natural function.

Peeling down to my individuality is filled with pitfalls, and I am sometimes powerless against the tension. Often I still wander in the dark like a refugee, knowing not where I am going. Yet this life of relocating in my dreams gives me the sense of being a real survivor. I have acquired the heart of a child, forever plunged into unfamiliar experiences, asking who I am, and why, as I stretch into new attitudes.

I had thought that healing meant that my conflicts would cease, but periodic anxiety and depression persist. I feel the inner pull in opposite directions. Occasionally this renders me hopeless, caring about nothing except relief, and I struggle to accept its necessity, glad to come through the darkness without panic. I can now see the interplay of light and dark, with neither dominating the other. As I witness this subjectively and objectively, I no longer fight it. Paradoxically, peace eventually comes because my wounds themselves have been constant. I sit with them as quietly as possible, and indeed my saving grace is within, to be mined from the pain itself. This has led me to a deep appreciation of my humanity.

My daily struggles teach me to honor my process as expressed in my vow to serve Mary and her son. With the depth of gratitude first experienced when my dream ego made that promise, I appreciate the rhythm of following my dreams as the rhythm of my life.

Once I see the correspondences between inner and outer happenings, doubt that creeps in unawares turns into certainty. I live in Mystery's presence, and thus in the mystery of my own. To touch it within myself helps me imagine it in others as I step comfortably into my life, fed from the unconscious.

Having developed a profound loyalty to my images, I try to respond to their richness wherever they appear. I now know where to look for my answers, and finding them within brings great rewards. As my images knead themselves into my being, fresh insights result. My healing goes on, and I grow stronger in the trust of my psyche. Given the vastness and fluidity of the unconscious life, I will forever be chasing my wholeness, but the journey itself gives meaning to my life and life to the meaning.

The inner path often seems friendless, and I sometimes lose my bearings by running from the lonely periods. Nevertheless, once faced, the threat lessens. I do not usually have the opportunity to rejoice with others in the religious definition of ourselves, but I have done so by telling my soul's story.

Searching through my journals has revealed the mystery. This is what the wise dream woman with one eye pointing above and one pointing below had in mind when she told me to write. Strength for my life has come, in a large degree, from writing this story. Putting it down on paper has been essential to my psychological expansion and has enabled me to take responsibility for it.

With each rewrite, I have wept as the mystery slowly penetrated my consciousness, opening me to my life as a spiritual practice in and of itself. Following its thread takes energy, and I grant myself this precious gift of attention to my inner drama. In the way of Mystery, complete understanding hovers all around, but is ever elusive, ever renewed.

Bibliography

Carotenuto, Aldo. *The Spiral Way: A Woman's Healing Journey.* Toronto: Inner City Books, 1986.

Grimm Brothers. *The Complete Grimm's Fairy Tales.* New York: Pantheon Books, 1972.

Hesse, Herman. *Steppenwolf.* Intro. Joseph Mileck. New York: Holt, Rinehart and Winston, 1963.

Jung, C.G. *The Collected Works* (Bollingen Series XX). 20 vols. Trans. R.F.C. Hull. Ed. H. Read, M. Fordham, G. Adler, Wm. McGuire. Princeton: Princeton University Press, 1953-1979.

_____. *Seminar 1925.* Mimeographed Notes of Seminar (March 23-July 6, 1925). C.G. Jung Institute of Zurich.

Lägerkvist, Par. *The Dwarf.* Trans. Alexandra Dick. New York: Farrar, Strauss and Giroux, Inc., 1945.

Perera, Sylvia Brinton. *Descent to the Goddess: A Way of Initiation for Women.* Toronto: Inner City Books, 1981.

Qualls-Corbett, Nancy. *The Sacred Prostitute: Eternal Aspect of the Feminine.* Toronto: Inner City Books, 1988.

Russian Folktales. Trans. E.C. Elstob and Richard Barber. London: G. Bell and Sons, 1971.

Sharp, Daryl. *Digesting Jung: Food for the Journey.* Toronto: Inner City Books, 2001.

Stassinopoulos, Arianna, and Beny, Roloff. *The Gods of Greece.* New York: Harry N. Abrams, Inc., 1983.

Warner, Marina. *Alone of All Her Sex.* New York: Random House, 1983.

Woodman, Marion. *Addiction to Perfection: The Still Unravished Bride.* Toronto: Inner City Books, 1982.

_____. *The Pregnant Virgin: A Process of Psychological Transformation.* Toronto: Inner City Books, 1985.

Index

active imagination, 32-33
afraid for her life (dream), 136-138
air, 79
alchemical dictum, 97
aliens, 43
analysis/analyst/analytic, 8-11, 23, 27, 64, 94, 98, 109-110, 128-129, 142, 144, 147. *See also* psychotherapy
animals, 41
animus, 111
  as dwarf, 72-73, 128
  as gigolo god, 79
  negative, 58-60, 72-73, 77
  positive, 58-60
  as stranger, 59-60, 86
Ann, 39-40. *See also* child
Annunciation, 109. *See also* Virgin Mary
Aphrodite, 86, 119-120
archetypal/archetype(s), 7, 12, 25, 36, 42, 58-59, 80, 83, 86, 89, 91, 96-97, 120-121, 143
  dreams, 129
ass, 41-42

baby, 89. *See also* child
bathing, 118-120, 139
"Beauty and the Beast" (fairy tale), 59
bells, 133
bird, white, 111-112
  launching, dream of, 110-113

birthday celebration, dream of, 142-143
book, dream of, 8-9
body, 15, 23, 26, 28, 46-47, 53-54, 57, 80, 91, 113, 121-122, 131, 147
  and spirit, 101, 120, 142
bus, 49

car, 139
card for Paul, dream of, 83-84
cat, 42. *See also* tiger
child, 36-38, 39-40, 58, 68, 74, 121, 123-125, 130-131, 135, 137, 147. *See also* baby
choking, 90
Christ/Christianity, 10, 22, 42, 61, 74, 115, 128-129
church, dream of leaving, 41-47
Circe, 86
clay mirror, dream of, 63-66, 134
closet child, dream of, 36-40
clothes, 29-31, 84-85, 114, 116
  dream of, 29
cobwebs, 43
Coleridge, Samuel Taylor: *The Ancient Mariner,* 119
color symbolism, 96
complex(es), 54-55, 96, 123, 144-145
  mother, 56, 67
common(ness), 18, 24, 27, 31, 41, 96, 101, 103, 144
conscious, 9, 54, 67

Also by Nancy Qualls-Corbett in this Series

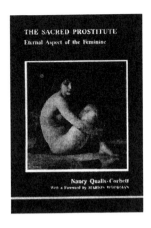

THE SACRED PROSTITUTE
Eternal Aspect of the Feminine

Foreword by Marion Woodman, author of *The Pregnant Virgin*
ISBN 0-919123-31-7. (1988) 20 illustrations. 176 pp. *Sewn* $18

The ancient connection between spirituality and passionate love has in modern times become lost to the depths of the unconscious, leaving a broad sense of dissatisfaction and boredom in relationships.

When the Goddess of Love was still honored, the sacred prostitute was virgin in the original sense of the word: one-in-herself—a person of deep integrity whose welcome for the stranger was radiant, self-confident and sensuous. Her raison d'être was to bring the goddess's love into direct contact with mankind.

In this union of opposites—masculine and feminine, spiritual and physical—the personal was transcended and the divine entered in. In those days, human sexuality and the religious attitude were inseparable.

This is an exhilarating book, solidly based on the psychological insights of C.G. Jung. It powerfully illustrates how our vitality and capacity for joy depend on restoring the soul of the sacred prostitute to its rightful place in our conscious understanding.

Partial List of Contents:
The Goddess and Her Virgin: Historical Background
Initiation into Womanhood
The Sacred Marriage Ritual
The Sacred Prostitute and Man's Anima
The Sacred Prostitute in Feminine Psychology
The Split Feminine: Mary Magdalene and the Virgin Mary
The Black Madonna
Restoration of the Soul

Other books in this Series especially for women

THE OWL WAS A BAKER'S DAUGHTER
Obesity, Anorexia Nervosa and the Repressed Feminine
Marion Woodman. ISBN 0-919123-03-1. (1980) 144pp. **18 illustrations** *Sewn* $16
Eye-opening insights into the body as mirror of the psyche in eating disorders and weight disturbances. Cases and practical procedures emphasize the integration of body and soul.

DESCENT TO THE GODDESS: A Way of Initiation for Women
Sylvia Brinton Perera. ISBN 0-919123-05-8. (1981) 112pp. *Sewn* $16
Pioneer study of the need for an inner female authority in a masculine-oriented society. Interprets the journey into the underworld of Inanna, Goddess of Heaven and Earth, to see Ereshkigal, her dark sister. So must modern women descend into their own depths.

THE CAT: A Tale of Feminine Redemption
Marie-Louise von Franz. ISBN 0-919123-84-8. (1999) 128pp. **Illustrated** *Sewn* $16
One by one von Franz unravels the symbolic threads in this Romanian story, from enchantment to beating, the ringing of bells, golden apples, somersaults and witches, and, throughout, the great themes of redemption and the union of opposites.

WORLD WEARY WOMAN: Her Wound and Transformation
Cara Barker. ISBN 0-919123-97-X. (2001) 160pp. *Sewn* $16
A World Weary Woman no longer finds joy in the struggle to achieve, suffering a disconnection from her feminine body wisdom and her creativity. Her task is to find a way of living authentically that allows her to express what awakens her heart.

COMING TO AGE: The Croning Years and Late-Life Transformation
Jane R. Prétat. ISBN 0-919123-63-5. (1994) 144pp. *Sewn* $16
A comprehensive overview of inner events and creative possibilities during the years after middle age. Explores the tasks and potential rewards of this period, with special reference to the Demeter-Persephone myth.

THE PREGNANT VIRGIN: A Process of Psychological Transformation
Marion Woodman. ISBN 0-919123-20-1. (1985) 208pp. **28 illustrations** *Sewn* $18
"The woman who is virgin, one-in-herself, does what she does not for power or out of the desire to please, but because what she does is true." Here is writing with a thinking heart, blending art, literature, religion and case material. Another modern classic.

ANIMUS AETERNUS: Exploring the Inner Masculine
Deldon Anne McNeely. ISBN 0-919123-50-3. (1991) 192pp. *Sewn* $18
Combining theory with soul-made truths found in the poetry of Sylvia Plath, Adrienne Rich, Teresa of Avalon, Emily Dickinson, Mary Oliver and many more, the author illumines the role of every woman's lifelong companion.

Studies in Jungian Psychology
by Jungian Analysts

Quality Paperbacks

Prices and payment in $US (except in Canada, $Cdn)

1. The Secret Raven: Conflict and Transformation
Daryl Sharp (Toronto). ISBN 0-919123-00-7. 128 pp. $16

2. The Psychological Meaning of Redemption Motifs in Fairy Tales
Marie-Louise von Franz (Zürich). ISBN 0-919123-01-5. 128 pp. $16

3. On Divination and Synchronicity: The Psychology of Meaningful Chance
Marie-Louise von Franz (Zürich). ISBN 0-919123-02-3. 128 pp. $16

4. The Owl Was a Baker's Daughter: Obesity, Anorexia and the Repressed Feminine Marion Woodman (Toronto). ISBN 0-919123-03-1. 144 pp. $16

5. Alchemy: An Introduction to the Symbolism and the Psychology
Marie-Louise von Franz (Zürich). ISBN 0-919123-04-X. 288 pp. $20

6. Descent to the Goddess: A Way of Initiation for Women
Sylvia Brinton Perera (New York). ISBN 0-919123-05-8. 112 pp. $16

7. The Psyche as Sacrament: A Comparative Study of C.G. Jung and Paul Tillich John P. Dourley (Ottawa). ISBN 0-919123-06-6. 128 pp. $16

8. Border Crossings: Carlos Castaneda's Path of Knowledge
Donald Lee Williams (Boulder). ISBN 0-919123-07-4. 160 pp. $16

9. Narcissism and Character Transformation: The Psychology of Narcissistic Character Disorders
Nathan Schwartz-Salant (New York). ISBN 0-919123-08-2. 192 pp. $18

10. Rape and Ritual: A Psychological Study
Bradley A. Te Paske (Santa Barbara). ISBN 0-919123-09-0. 160 pp. $16

11. Alcoholism and Women: The Background and the Psychology
Jan Bauer (Montreal). ISBN 0-919123-10-4. 144 pp. $16

12. Addiction to Perfection: The Still Unravished Bride
Marion Woodman (Toronto). ISBN 0-919123-11-2. 208 pp. $18pb/$25hc

13. Jungian Dream Interpretation: A Handbook of Theory and Practice
James A. Hall, M.D. (Dallas). ISBN 0-919123-12-0. 128 pp. $16

14. The Creation of Consciousness: Jung's Myth for Modern Man
Edward F. Edinger (Los Angeles). ISBN 0-919123-13-9. 128 pp. $16

15. The Analytic Encounter: Transference and Human Relationship
Mario Jacoby (Zürich). ISBN 0-919123-14-7. 128 pp. $16

16. Change of Life: Dreams and the Menopause
Ann Mankowitz (Ireland). ISBN 0-919123-15-5. 128 pp. $16

17. The Illness That We Are: A Jungian Critique of Christianity
John P. Dourley (Ottawa). ISBN 0-919123-16-3. 128 pp. $16

18. Hags and Heroes: A Feminist Approach to Jungian Psychotherapy with Couples Polly Young-Eisendrath (Philadelphia). ISBN 0-919123-17-1. 192 pp. $18

19. Cultural Attitudes in Psychological Perspective
Joseph L. Henderson, M.D. (San Francisco). ISBN 0-919123-18-X. 128 pp. $16

20. The Vertical Labyrinth: Individuation in Jungian Psychology
Aldo Carotenuto (Rome). ISBN 0-919123-19-8. 144 pp. $16

44. The Dream Story
Donald Broadribb (Baker's Hill, Australia). ISBN 0-919123-45-7. 256 pp. $20

45. The Rainbow Serpent: Bridge to Consciousness
Robert L. Gardner (Toronto). ISBN 0-919123-46-5. 128 pp. $16

46. Circle of Care: Clinical Issues in Jungian Therapy
Warren Steinberg (New York). ISBN 0-919123-47-3. 160 pp. $16

47. Jung Lexicon: A Primer of Terms & Concepts
Daryl Sharp (Toronto). ISBN 0-919123-48-1. 160 pp. $16

48. Body and Soul: The Other Side of Illness
Albert Kreinheder (Los Angeles). ISBN 0-919123-49-X. 112 pp. $16

49. Animus Aeternus: Exploring the Inner Masculine
Deldon Anne McNeely (Lynchburg, VA). ISBN 0-919123-50-3. 192 pp. $18

50. Castration and Male Rage: The Phallic Wound
Eugene Monick (Scranton, PA). ISBN 0-919123-51-1. 144 pp. $16

51. Saturday's Child: Encounters with the Dark Gods
Janet O. Dallett (Seal Harbor, WA). ISBN 0-919123-52-X. 128 pp. $16

52. The Secret Lore of Gardening: Patterns of Male Intimacy
Graham Jackson (Toronto). ISBN 0-919123-53-8. 160 pp. $16

53. The Refiner's Fire: Memoirs of a German Girlhood
Sigrid R. McPherson (Los Angeles). ISBN 0-919123-54-6. 208 pp. $18

54. Transformation of the God-Image: Jung's *Answer to Job*
Edward F. Edinger (Los Angeles). ISBN 0-919123-55-4. 144 pp. $16

55. Getting to Know You: The Inside Out of Relationship
Daryl Sharp (Toronto). ISBN 0-919123-56-2. 128 pp. $16

56. A Strategy for a Loss of Faith: Jung's Proposal
John P. Dourley (Ottawa). ISBN 0-919123-57-0. 144 pp. $16

57. Close Relationships: Family, Friendship, Marriage
Eleanor Bertine (New York). ISBN 0-919123-58-9. 160 pp. $16

58. Conscious Femininity: Interviews with Marion Woodman
Introduction by Marion Woodman (Toronto). ISBN 0-919123-59-7. 160 pp. $16

59. The Middle Passage: From Misery to Meaning in Midlife
James Hollis (Houston). ISBN 0-919123-60-0. 128 pp. $16

60. The Living Room Mysteries: Patterns of Male Intimacy, Book 2
Graham Jackson (Toronto). ISBN 0-919123-61-9. 144 pp. $16

61. Chicken Little: The Inside Story *(A Jungian Romance)*
Daryl Sharp (Toronto). ISBN 0-919123-62-7. 128 pp. $16

62. Coming To Age: The Croning Years and Late-Life Transformation
Jane R. Prétat (Providence, RI). ISBN 0-919123-63-5. 144 pp. $16

63. Under Saturn's Shadow: The Wounding and Healing of Men
James Hollis (Houston). ISBN 0-919123-64-3. 144 pp. $16

Discounts: any 3-5 books, 10%; 6-9 books, 20%; 10 or more, 25%
Add Postage/Handling: 1-2 books, $3; 3-4 books, $5; 5-9 books, $10; 10 or more, free

Write or phone for free Catalogue of **over 100 titles** and **Jung at Heart** newsletter

INNER CITY BOOKS

Box 1271, Station Q, Toronto, ON M4T 2P4, Canada   (416) 927-0355